Berlitz®

Brazilian
Portuguese

phrase book & dictionary

Berlitz Publishing
New York   London   Singapore

Contacting the Editors
Every effort has been made to provide accurate information in this publication, but changes are inevitable. The publisher cannot be responsible for any resulting loss, inconvenience or injury. We would appreciate it if readers would call our attention to any errors or outdated information. We also welcome your suggestions; if you come across a relevant expression not in our phrase book, please contact us at: **comments@berlitzpublishing.com**

Printed in China

Editor: Helen Fanthorpe
Translation: updated by Wordbank
Cover Design: Rebeka Davies
Interior Design: Beverley Speight

Picture Researcher: Beverley Speight
Cover Photos: Shutterstock.
Interior Photos: All photos Yadid Levy/APA except Britta Jaschinski/APA p47; Bev Speight/APA p148; iStockphoto p23,82,145,154,155,161,166

Distribution
UK, Ireland and Europe
Apa Publications (UK) Ltd
sales@insightguides.com
United States and Canada
Ingram Publisher Services
ips@ingramcontent.com
Australia and New Zealand
Woodslane
info@woodslane.com.au
Southeast Asia
Apa Publications (SN) Pte
singaporeoffice@insightguides.com

Worldwide
Apa Publications (UK) Ltd
sales@insightguides.com

Special Sales, Content Licensing, and CoPublishing
Discounts available for bulk quantities. We can create special editions, personalized jackets, and corporate imprints. sales@insightguides.com; www.insightguides.biz

Contents

Food & Drink

People

Leisure Time

Special Requirements

In an Emergency

Dictionary

Pronunciation

This section is designed to make you familiar with the sounds of Brazilian Portuguese using our simplified phonetic transcription. You'll find the pronunciation of the Brazilian Portuguese letters and sounds explained below, together with their 'imitated' equivalents. This system is used throughout the phrase book; simply read the pronunciation as if it were English, noting any special rules below.

Please note that any syllables that should be stressed are indicated by underlining in the phonetics.

Brazilian Portuguese has four accent marks; acute (´), grave (`), circumflex (^), and tilde (~). Accent marks are used to indicate a stressed syllable, or to distinguish between words with the same spelling but with a different pronunciation and meaning: for example, **é** pronounced *eh* (meaning is) and **e** pronounced *ee* (meaning and).

Consonants

Letter	Approximate Pronunciation	Symbol	Example	Pronunciation
b	1. as in English	**b**	**bota**	*baw·tuh*
	2. between vowels, as in English but softer	**b**	**bebida**	*beh·bee·duh*
c	1. before e or i, like s in same	**s**	**centro**	*sehn·troh*
	2. like k in kit	**k**	**como**	*koh·moh*
ç	like s in same	**s**	**cabeça**	*kuh·beh·suh*
ch	like sh in shower	**sh**	**chave**	*shahvd*

Letter	Approximate Pronunciation	Symbol	Example	Pronunciation
d	1. as in English	**d**	**diário**	_dee·ah·ree·oo_
	2. like th in theater	**th**	**medo**	_meh·thoo_
g	1. before e or i, like s in pleasure	**zs**	**gelo**	_zseh·loo_
	2. before a, o or u, as in English	**g**	**guerra**	_geh·rruh_
h	always silent		**história**	_ee·staw·ree·uh_
j	like s in pleasure	**zs**	**juiz**	_zsoo·eezs_
l	1. as in English	**l**	**luz**	_looz_
	2. before h (lh), like ll in millions	**ly**	**milho**	_mee·lyoo_
m	1. as in English	**m**	**câmera**	_cuh·meh·ruh_
	2. at the end of a word, m is nasalized: see p10			
n	1. as in English	**n**	**caneta**	_kuh·neh·tah_
	2. before h (nh), like ny in canyon	**ny**	**banho**	_buh·nyoo_
qu	1. before e and i, like k in kite	**k**	**quente**	_kint_
	2. before a and o like qu in queen	**kw**	**qualidade**	_kwah·lee·dahd_
r	1. strongly trilled	**rr**	**rio**	_rree·oo_
	2. lightly trilled	**r**	**para**	_puh·ruh_
s	1. like s in same	**s**	**sua**	_soo·uh_
	2. between vowels, like z in zebra	**z**	**camisa**	_kuh·mee·zuh_

Letter	Approximate Pronunciation	Symbol	Example	Pronunciation
x	1. like sh in sheep	**sh**	**peixe**	*paysh*
	2. like s in same	**s**	**próximo**	*praw·see·moo*
	3. like z in lazy	**z**	**exame**	*ee·zuhm*

Letters f, m, p, t and z are pronounced as in English. Letters k, w and y are used only in foreign loan words.

Vowels

Letter	Approximate Pronunciation	Symbol	Example	Pronunciation
a, ã, â	like a in about	**uh**	**anos**	*uh·nooz*
á, à	like a in father	**ah**	**farmácia**	*fuhr·mah·see·uh*
e	1. like e in get	**eh**	**esta**	*eh·stuh*
	2. like ee in eel	**ee**	**exame**	*ee·zuhm*
	3. silent at the end of a word		**leite**	*layt*
	4. occasionally, like i in inn	**i**	**antes**	*ahn·tis*
	5. when combined with the letter i, like ay in say	**ay**	**leite**	*layt*
é	like e in get	**eh**	**esta**	*eh·stuh*
ê	like i in inn	**i**	**mês**	*miz*
i, í	like ee in eel	**ee**	**sim**	*seeng*
o	1. like au in caught	**au**	**onda**	*aun·duh*
	2. at the end of a word, like oo in boo	**oo**	**gato**	*gah·too*
oi	like oy in coy	**oy**	**doi**	*doy*

Letter	Approximate Pronunciation	Symbol	Example	Pronunciation
ó	like aw in paw	**aw**	**história**	*ee·staw·ree·uh*
ô	like u in put	**oah**	**avô**	*uh·voah*
u	1. like oo in boo	**oo**	**uva**	*oo·vuh*
	2. silent after g and q		**guerra**	*geh·rruh*
ú	like oo in boo	**oo**	**úmido**	*oo·mee·thoo*

When a vowel has an accent, you must stress the syllable in the word that contains the accented vowel.

Nasal Sounds

Some nasal sounds are produced when a vowel is followed by the letter **m**. This nasal sound is also found when a combination of certain vowels are used (**ãe**, **ão**, **õe**). These nasal sounds produce either an *ng* sound (e.g., tying) or an *oam* sound (e.g., foam) with the speaker barely pronouncing the g or m.

Letter	Approximate Pronunciation	Symbol	Example	Pronunciation
ãe	like ayin in saying	**eng**	**mãe**	*meng*
ão	like oam in foam	**ohm**	**cão**	*kohm*
õe	like oing in boing	**oing**	**milhões**	*mee·lyoings*
am	at the end of a word, like oam in foam otherwise not nasal: see page 8	**ohm**	**falam**	*fah·loam*
om	like ong in gong	**ohng**	**som**	*sohng*

Letter	Approximate Pronunciation	Symbol	Example	Pronunciation
em	like aying in saying	**eng**	**bem**	*beng*
im	like ing in tying	**ing**	**assim**	*uh·sing*

There are some differences in both the vocabulary and pronunciation of the Portuguese spoken in Portugal and that spoken in Brazil, although people in both countries can easily understand one another. This book is specifically designed for travelers to Brazil.

How to use this Book

Sometimes you see two alternatives separated by a slash. Choose the one that's right for your situation.

ESSENTIAL

Where's the pharmacy [chemist]?	**Onde fica a farmácia?** aund fee-kuh uh fuhr-mah-see-uh
What time does the pharmacy open/close?	**A que horas abre/fecha a farmácia?** uh keh aw-ruhz ah-breh/feh-shuh uh fuhr-mah-see-uh
What would you recommend for...?	**O que é que me recomenda para...?** oo keh eh keh meh reh-koo-mehn-duh puh-ruh...

Words you may see are shown in YOU MAY SEE boxes.

YOU MAY SEE...

CHEGADAS	arrivals
PARTIDAS	departures
ENTREGA DE BAGAGEM	baggage claim

Any of the words or phrases listed can be plugged into the sentence below.

Tickets

When's...	**A que horas é... para...?** uh kee aw-ruhz eh... puh-ruh
the (first) bus to	**o (primeiro) ônibus** uh pree-may-roo aw-nee-boos
the (next) flight	**o (próximo) vôo** oo (praw-see-moo) vau-oo
the (last) train	**o (último) trem** oo (ool-tee-moo) treng

Brazilian Portuguese phrases appear in purple.

Read the simplified pronunciation as if it were English. For more on pronunciation, see page 7.

Conversation

Hello.	**Oi.** *au·hee*
How are you?	**Tudo bem?** *Too·duh beng*
Fine, thanks.	**Bem, obrigado m /obrigada f.** *behm aw·bree·gah·doo/ aw·bree·gah·duh*
Excuse me!	**Desculpe!** *dehz·kool·peh*

For Numbers, see page 173.

Related phrases can be found by going to the page number indicated.

When different gender forms apply, the masculine form is followed by *m*; feminine by *f*

Parking can be difficult in big cities. Always lock your car and never leave anything in sight (even if you consider it not valuable) as it can encourage break-ins.

Information boxes contain relevant country, culture and language tips.

Expressions you may hear are shown in You May Hear boxes.

YOU MAY HEAR...

O que deseja? *oo keh deh·zeh·zsuh*	What would you like?
Recomendo... *reh·koo·mehn·doo...*	I recommend...
Bom apetite. *bohng uh·peh·tee·teh*	Enjoy your meal.

Color-coded side bars identify each section of the book.

Survival

Arrival & Departure

ESSENTIAL

I'm on vacation [holiday]/business.	**Estou de férias/em negócios.** *ee·stawoo deh feh·ree·uhz/eng neh·gaw·see·yooz*
I'm going to…	**Vou para…** *vawoo puh·ruh…*
I'm staying at the… Hotel.	**Estou no hotel…** *ee·stawoo noo aw·tehl…*

YOU MAY HEAR…

O seu bilhete/passaporte. *oo sehoo bee·lyeht /pah·suh·pawrt*
Your ticket/passport, please.

Qual é o propósito de sua visita? *kwahl eh oo prau·paw·zee·too deh soo·uh vee·zee·tuh*
What's the purpose of your visit?

Onde está ficando? *aund ee·stah uh fee·kuhn·doo*
Where are you staying?

Quanto tempo vai ficar? *kwuhn·too tehm·poo veye fee·kahr*
How long are you staying?

Com quem está? *kohm keng ee·stah*
Who are you with?

Border Control

I'm just passing through.	**Estou só de passagem.** *ee·stawoo saw deh puh·sah·zheng*
I would like to declare…	**Queria declarar…** *keh·ree·uh deh·kluh·rahr…*
I have nothing to declare.	**Não tenho nada a declarar.** *nohm teh·nyoo nah·duh uh deh·kluh·rahr*

YOU MAY HEAR...

Tem alguma coisa a declarar?
teng ahl·goo·muh koy·zuh uh deh·kluh·rahr

Tem de pagar direitos [alfandegários] nisto. *teng deh puh·gahr dee·ray·tooz [uhl·fuhn·deh·gah·ree·ooz] nee·stoo*

Abra esta mala, por favor. *ah·bruh eh·stah mah.lah poor fuh·vaur*

Do you have anything to declare?
You must pay duty on this.

Please open this bag.

YOU MAY SEE...

ALFÂNDEGA	customs
MERCADORIA SEM TAXAS	duty-free goods
ARTIGOS A DECLARAR	goods to declare
NADA A DECLARAR	nothing to declare
CONTROLE DE PASSAPORTES	passport control
POLÍCIA	police

Money

ESSENTIAL

Where's...?	**Onde é...?** *aund eh...*
the ATM	**o caixa eletrônico** *oo keye·shuh uhleh·trau·nee·kau*
the bank	**o banco** *oo buhn·koo*
the currency exchange office	**o câmbio** *oo kuhm·bee·oo*
What time does the bank open/close?	**A que horas o banco abre/fecha?** *uh keh aw·ruhz oo buhn·koo ah·breh/feh·shuh*

16

I'd like to change dollars/pounds/ euros into reais. **Queria trocar dólares/libras/euros em reais.** *keh·ree·uh troo·kahr daw·luhrz/lee·bruhz/ ehoo·rooz eng rree·eyez*

I want to cash some traveler's checks [cheques]. **Quero trocar cheques de viagem.** *keh·roo troo·kahr sheh·kehz deh vee·ah·zseng*

At the Bank

Can I exchange foreign currency/get a cash advance here? **Posso trocar moedas estrangeiras/ obter dinheiro a crédito aqui?** *paw·soo troo·kahr moo·eh·duhz ee·struhn·zsay·ruhz au·btehr dee·nyay·roo uh kreh·dee·too uh·kee*

What's the exchange rate? **Quanto está o câmbio?** *kwuhn·too ee·stah oo kuhm·bee·oo*

How much commission do you charge? **Quanto cobram de comissão?** *kwuhn·too kaw·brohm deh koo·mee·sohm*

I think there's a mistake. **Penso que há um erro.** *pehn·soo keh ah oong eh·rroo*

I've lost my traveler's checks [cheques]. **Perdio meu talão de cheques.** *pehr.dee oo mehoo tah.lohm deh sheh·kehz*

My card was lost. **O meu cartão foi perdido.** *oo mehoo kuhr·tohm foy pehr·dee·thoo*

My credit card has been stolen. **Roubaram o meu cartão de crédito.** *raw·bah·rohm oo mehoo kuhr·tohm deh kreh·dee·too*

My credit card doesn't work. **O meu cartão de crédito não funciona.** *oo mehoo kuhr·tohm deh kreh·dee·too nohm foon·see·au·nuh*

The ATM ate my card. **O caixa eletrônico ficou com o meu cartão.** *uh cah·ee·shah uh·leh·trau·nee·kau fee·kawoo kaum oo mehoo kuhr·tohm*

For Numbers, see page 173.

YOU MAY SEE...

INSERIR O CARTÃO	insert card here
CANCELAR	cancel
APAGAR	clear
CONFIRMAR	enter
PIN	PIN
RETIRAR DINHEIRO	withdraw funds
DA CONTA CORRENTE	from checking [current] account
DA CONTA DE POUPANÇA	from savings account
RECIBO	receipt

Currency exchange offices (**Câmbio**) can be found in most Brazilian tourist centers; they generally stay open longer than banks, especially during the summer season. Travel agencies and hotels are other places where you can exchange money, but the rate will not be as good. In heavy tourist areas, you can also find currency exchange machines/ATMs on the streets. Of course, you should use caution when exchanging/withdrawing money on the street, especially in cities where crime rates are high. Remember to take your passport with you when you want to change money.

YOU MAY SEE...

The currency in Brazil is the **real (R$)**, plural **reais**, divided into 100 **centavos**.
Coins: 1, 5, 10, 25, 50 **centavos**; 1 **R$**
Notes: 2, 5, 10, 20, 50, 100 **R$**

ESSENTIAL

How do I get to the city center?	**Como vou para o centro da cidade?** _kau•moo vawoo puh•ruh oo sehn•troo duh see•dahd_
Where's...?	**Onde é...?** _aund eh..._
the airport	**o aeroporto** _oo uh•eh•rau•paur•too_
the train station	**a estação ferroviária** _uh ee•stuh•sohm feh•rroo•vee•ah•ree•uh_
the bus station	**a estação de ônibus** _uh ee•stuh•sohm deh aw•nee•boos_
the metro [underground] station	**a estação de metrô** _uh ee•stuh•sohm deh meh•troo_
How far is it?	**A que distância fica?** _uh keh dee•stuhn•see•uh fee•kuh_
Where can I buy tickets?	**Onde posso comprar bilhetes?** _aund paw•soo kaum•prahr bee•lyehtz_
A one-way/return-trip ticket to...	**Um bilhete de ida/de ida e volta para...** _oong bee•lyeht deh ee•thuh/deh ee•thuh ee vaul•tuh puh•ruh..._
How much?	**Quanto custa?** _kwuhn•too koo•stuh_
Are there any discounts?	**Há descontos?** _ah dehs•caun•tooz_
Which...?	**Qual...?** _kwahl..._
gate	**porta** _port•uh_
line	**linha** _lee•nyuh_
platform	**plataforma** _plah•tuh•fawr•muh_
Where can I get a taxi?	**Onde posso pegar um táxi?** _aund paw•soo peh•gahr oong tahk•see_

Please take me to this address.	**Leve-me neste endereço.** *leh•veh•meh nehst ehn•deh•reh•soo*
Where can I rent a car?	**Onde posso alugar um carro?** *aund paw•soo uh•loo•gahr oong kah•rroo*
Could I have a map?	**Pode me dar um mapa?** *pawd meh dahr oong mah•puh*

Tickets

When's...to...?	**A que horas é...para...?** *uh kee aw•ruhz eh... puh•ruh...*
the (first) bus	**o (primeiro) ônibus** *uh (pree•may•ruh) aw•nee•boos*
the (next) flight	**o (próximo) vôo** *oo (praw•see•moo) vau•oo*
the (last) train	**o (último) trem** *oo (ool•tee•moo) treng*
Where can I buy tickets?	**Onde posso comprar bilhetes?** *aund paw•soo kaum•prahr bee•lyehtz*
One/Two ticket(s), please.	**Um bilhete/Dois bilhetes, por favor.** *oong bee•lyeht/doyz bee•lyehtz poor fuh•vaur*
For today/tomorrow.	**Para hoje/amanhã.** *puh•ruh auzseh/uh•muh•nyuh*
A...ticket.	**Um bilhete...** *oong bee•lyeht...*
one-way	**de ida** *deh ee•thuh*
return-trip	**de ida e volta** *deh ee•thuh ee vaul•tuh*
first-class	**em primeira classe** *eng pree•may•ruh klah•she*
	business class
economy class	**em classe econômica** *eng klah•seh eh•koo•naw•mee•kuh*
How much?	**Quanto custa?** *kwuhn•too koo•stuh*
Is there a discount for...?	**Há desconto para...?** *ah dehs•kaum•too puh•ruh...*
children	**crianças** *kree•uhn•suhz*
students	**estudantes** *ee•stoo•duhnts*
senior citizens	**idosos** *ee•daw•zooz*

tourists	**turistas** *too·ree·stuhz*
The express bus/express train, please.	**A ônibus expresso/o trem expresso, por favor.** *uh aw·nee·boos /oo treng ees·preh·soo, poor fuh·vaur*
The local bus/train, please.	**A ônibus/o trem local, por favor.** *uh aw·nee·boos /oo treng loo·kahl, poor fuh·vaur*
I have an e-ticket.	**Eu tenho um bilhete electrônico.** *ehoo <u>teh</u>·nyoo oong bee·<u>lyeht</u> ee·le·<u>tro</u>·<u>nee</u>·kuh*
Can I buy a ticket on the bus/train?	**Posso comprar o bilhete no ônibus/no trem?** *<u>paw</u>·soo kaum·<u>prahr</u> oo bee·<u>lyeht</u> noo <u>aw</u>·nee·boos/noo treng*
Do I have to stamp the ticket before boarding?	**Tenho de carimbar o bilhete antes de embarcar?** *teh·nyoo deh kuh·reem·bahr oo bee·lyeht uhnts deh ehm·buhr·kahr*
How long is this ticket valid?	**Até quando este bilhete é válido?** *uh·teh kwuhn doo ehst bee·lyeht eh vah·lee·doo*
Can I return on the same ticket?	**Posso voltar com o mesmo bilhete?** *paw·soo vaul·tuhr kaum oo mehz·moo bee·lyeht*
I'd like to...my reservation.	**Queria...a minha reserva.** *keh·<u>ree</u>·uh...uh <u>mee</u>·nyuh reh·<u>zehr</u>·vuh*
cancel	**cancelar** *kuhn·seh·<u>lahr</u>*
change	**mudar** *moo·<u>dahr</u>*
confirm	**confirmar** *kaum·feer·<u>mahr</u>*

Plane

Airport Transfer

How much is a taxi to the airport?	**Quanto custa um táxi para o aeroporto?** *kwuhn·too koo·stuh oong tahk·see puh·ruh oo uh·eh·rau·paur·too*
To...Airport, please.	**Ao aeroporto de..., por favor.** *ahoo uh·eh·rau·paur·too deh...poor fuh·vaur*
My airline is...	**A minha linha aérea é...** *uh mee·nyuh lee·nyuh ah·ehr·ee·uh eh...*
My flight leaves at...	**O meu vôo parte às...** *oo meeoo vau·oo pahr·teh ahz...*
I'm in a hurry.	**Estou com pressa.** *ee·stawoo kaum preh·suh*
Can you take an alternate route?	**Pode tomar um caminho alternativo?** *pawd too·mahr oong kuh·mee·nyoo ahl·tehr·nah·tee·vuh*
Can you drive faster/ slower?	**Pode dirigir mais rápido/devagar?** *pawd dee·ree·jeer meyez rah·pee·thoo/deh·vuh·gahr*

For Time, see page 175.

YOU MAY SEE...

CHEGADAS	arrivals
PARTIDAS	departures
ENTREGA DE BAGAGEM	baggage claim
VÔOS DOMÉSTICOS	domestic flights
VÔOS INTERNACIONAIS	international flights
BALCÃO DE CHECK-IN	check-in desk
REGISTRO DE BILHETE ELECTRÔNICO	e-ticket check-in
PORTÕES DE PARTIDA	departure gates

:50 13:02 **GUARULHOS** Pouso
:55 12:56 **BRASÍLIA** Confirmado
03 13:10 **GUARULHOS** Aeronave no Pá
20 13:07 **BRASÍLIA** Confirmado
0 13:10 **BARREIRAS** Confirmado
SÃO PAULO Confirmado
13:15 **R DE JANEIRO** Cia. não Informo
13:15 **FORTALEZA** Confirmado
13:40 **SÃO PAULO** Confirmado
3:35 **PETROL** Confirma

YOU MAY HEAR...

Que linha aérea voam? keh *lee*·nyuh *ah*·*eh*·ree·uh *vau*·ohm	What airline are you flying?
Doméstico ou internacional? thoo·*meh*·stee·koo awoo een·tehr·*nuh*·seeoo·nahl	Domestic or international?
Que terminal? keh tehr·mee·*nahl*	What terminal?

Checking In

Where is the check-in counter?	**Onde é o check in?** aund eh oo check in
My name is...	**Meu nome é...** mehoo *nau*·mee eh...
I'm going to...	**Vou para...** vauoo *puh*·ruh...
I have...	**Tenho...** teh·nyoo...
one suitcase	**uma mala** oo·muh mah·luh
two suitcases	**duás malas** thoo·uhz mah·luhs
one piece of hand luggage	**uma bagagem de mão** oo·muh buh·*gah*·zsen deh mohm

How much luggage is allowed?	**Quantas bagagens são permitidas?** *kwuhn•tuhz buh•gah•zsengs sohm pehr•mee•tee•thuhs*
Is that pounds or kilos?	**Isso está em libras ou quilos?** *ee•soo ee•stah eng lee•bruhz awoo kee•laes*
Which terminal/gate does flight…leave from?	**Qual é o terminal para o vôo/a porta do vôo para…?** *kwahl eh oo tehr•mee•nahl puh•ruh oo vau•oo/uh pawr•tuhz thoo vau•oo puh•ruh…*
I'd like a window/ an aisle seat.	**Queria um lugar na janela/no corredor.** *keh•ree•uh oong loo•gahr nah zsuh•neh•luh/ noo koo•rreh•daur*
When do we leave/ arrive?	**Quando vamos partir/chegar?** *kwuhn•doo vuh•mooz puhr•teer/shee•gahr*
Is flight…delayed?	**Há atraso no vôo…?** *ah uh•trah•zoo noo vau•oo…*
How late will it be?	**Qual é o atraso?** *kwahl eh oo uh•trah•zoo*

Luggage

Where is/are…?	**Onde é/são…?** *aund eh/sohm…*
the luggage trolleys	**os carrinhos** *ooz kuh•rree•nyos*
the luggage lockers	**os armários de bagagem** *ooz ahr•mah•ree•uhz deh buh•gah•zseng*
the baggage claim	**o depósito de bagagem** *oo deh•paw•zee•too deh buh•gah•zseng*
My luggage has been lost.	**Perdi a minha bagagem.** *pehr•dee uh mee•nyuh buh•gah•zseng*
My luggage has been stolen.	**Roubaram a minha bagagem.** *raw•bah•rohm uh mee•nyuh buh•gah•zseng*
My suitcase was damaged.	**A minha mala foi danificada.** *uh mee•nyuh mah•luh foy deh•nee•fee•kah•thuh*

YOU MAY HEAR...

Próximo! _praw•see•moo_   Next!

O seu bilhete/passaporte, por favor.   Your ticket/passport,
oo sehoo bee•lyet/pah•suh•pawrt poor fuh•vaur   please.

Tem bagagem para despachar?   Are you checking any
teng buh•gah•zseng puh•ruh dehs•puh•shahr   luggage?

Tem excesso de peso na sua bagagem.   You have excess baggage.
teng eh•zeh•soo deh peh•zoo nuh soo•uh
buh•gah•zseng

Isso é muito volumoso para   That's too large for a
bagagem de mão. _ee•soo eh_   carry-on [to carry on
moo.ee.too vaw•loo•mau•zoo   board]._
puh•ruh buh•gah•zseng deh mohm

Foi o senhor _m_ /a senhora _f_ quem fez   Did you pack these bags
as malas? _foy oo see•nyaur/_   yourself?
uh see•nyau•ruh keng fehz uhs mah•luhs

Alguém lhe deu alguma coisa para   Did anyone give you
transportar? _ahl•geng lyeh dehoo_   anything to carry?
ahl•goo•muh coy•zuh puh•ruh truhns•pawr•tahr

Tire tudo dos bolsos. _tee•reh too•thoo dooz_   Empty your pockets.
bawl•sooz

Tire os seus sapatos. _tee•reh ooz sehooz_   Take off your shoes.
suh•pah•tooz

Estamos a embarcar o vôo... _ee•stuh•mooz_   Now boarding flight...
uh eng•buhr•kahr oo vau•oo...

Finding your Way

Where is/are…?	**Onde é/são…?** *aund eh/sohm*
the currency exchange office	**o câmbio** *oo kuhm•bee•oo*
the car hire	**o aluguel de carros** *oo uh•loo•gehl deh kah•rrooz*
the exit	**a saída** *uh suh•ee•thuh*
the taxis	**os táxis** *ooz tahk•seez*
Is there…into town?	**Há…para o centro?** *ah… puh•ruh oo sehn•troo*
a bus	**um ônibus** *oong aw•nee•boos*
a train	**um trem** *oong treng*
a metro [underground]	**um metrô** *oong meh•troo*

For Asking Directions, see page 36.

Train

| Where's the nearest train station? | **Onde está a estação de trens mais próxima?** *aund ee•stah uh ee•stuh•sohm deh trengs meyez praw•see•muh* |
| How far is it? | **A que distância fica?** *uh keh dee•stuhn•see•uh fee•kuh* |

Where is/are...?	**Onde está/são...?**
	aund ee·stah/sohm...
the ticket office	**a bilheteria** *uh bee·lyeht·eh·ree·uh*
the information desk	**as informações**
	uhz een·foor·muh·soingz
the luggage lockers	**os armários de bagagem**
	ooz ahr·mah·ree·uhz deh buh·gah·zseng
the platforms	**as plataformas** *uhz plah·tuh·fawr·muhz*
Could I have a schedule [timetable], please?	**Queria um horário, por favor.** *keh·ree·uh oong aw·rah·ree·oo poor fuh·vaur*
How long is the trip?	**Quanto tempo demora a viagem?**
	kwuhn·too tehm·poo deh·maw·ruh uh vee·ah·zseng
Is it a direct train?	**É um trem directo?**
	eh oong treng dee·reh·too
Do I have to change trains?	**Tenho de mudar de trem?**
	teh·nyoo deh moo·dahr deh treng
Is the train on time?	**O trem chega a horas?**
	oo treng shee·gah uh aw·ruhz

For Tickets, see page 20.

Departures

Which track [platform] for the train to...?	**De que plataforma parte o trem para...?** *deh keh plah·tuh·fawr·muh pahrt oo treng puh·ruh...*
Is this the track [platform] to...?	**É daqui que parte o trem para...?** *eh duh·kee keh pahrt oo treng puh·ruh...*
Where is track [platform]...?	**Onde é a plataforma...?** *aund eh uh plah·tuh·fawr·muh...*
Where do I change for...?	**Onde é que mudo para...?** *aund eh keh moo·thoo puh·ruh...*

On Board

Is this seat taken?	**Este lugar está ocupado?** *ehst loo-gahr ee-stah aw-koo-pah-thoo*
Can I sit here/ open the window?	**Posso sentar aqui/abrir a janela?** *paw-soo sehn-tahr uh-kee/ah-breer uh zsuh-neh-luh*
That's my seat.	**Esse é o meu lugar.** *eh-seh eh oo mehoo loo-gahr*
Here's my reservation.	**Aqui está a minha reserva.** *uh-kee ee-stah uh mee-nyuh reh-zehr-vuh*

YOU MAY SEE...

PARA AS LINHAS	to the platforms
INFORMAÇÕES	information
RESERVAS	reservations
SALA DE ESPERA	waiting room
CHEGADAS	arrivals
PARTIDAS	departures

In Brazil the rail network is quite small. The Brazilian railway, **Estrada de Ferro Central do Brasil (E.F.C.B.)**, offers few passenger services. The São Paulo–Rio de Janeiro night journey is comfortable but long and expensive.

Bus

Where's the bus station?	**Onde é a estação de ônibus?** *aund eh uh ee·stuh·<u>sohm</u> deh <u>aw</u>·nee·boos*
How far is it?	**A que distância fica?** *uh keh dee·<u>stuhn</u>·see·uh <u>fee</u>·kuh*
How do I get to…?	**Como se vai para…?** *<u>kau</u>·moo seh veye <u>puh</u>·ruh…*
Does the bus [coach] stop at…?	**O ônibus pára em…?** *uh oo <u>aw</u>·nee·boos <u>pah</u>·ruh eng…*
Could you tell me when to get off?	**Pode-me dizer quando devo sair?** *<u>paw</u>·deh meh dee·<u>zehr</u> <u>kwuhn</u>·doo <u>deh</u>·voo suh·<u>eer</u>*

YOU MAY HEAR…

Todos a bordo! *<u>toah</u>·<u>thooz</u> uh <u>baur</u>·thoo*	All aboard!
Bilhetes, por favor. *bee·<u>lyehtz</u> poor fuh·<u>vaur</u>*	Tickets, please.
Tem de mudar em… *teng deh moo·<u>dahr</u> eng…*	You have to change at…
A próxima parada… *uh <u>praw</u>·see·muh puh·<u>rah</u>·duh…*	Next stop…

Do I have to change buses?	**Tenho de mudar de autocarro [ônibus]?**
	teh•nyoo deh moo•dahr deh ahoo•too•kah•rroo [aw•nee•boos]
Stop here, please!	**Pare aqui, por favor!**
	pah•reh uh•kee poor fuh•vaur

For Tickets, see page 20.

Intercity buses are fairly cheap and comfortable, usually with air conditioning. If you are traveling overnight, look for **leitos**, buses with reclining seats, clean sheets and pillows. Tickets are available from bus stations (**rodoviárias**).

Metro

Where's the nearest metro [underground] station?	**Onde é a estação de metrô mais próxima?**
	aund eh uh ee•stuh•sohm deh meh•troo meyez praw•see•muh
Could I have a map of the subway [underground], please?	**Pode me dar um mapa do metrô, por favor?**
	pawd meh dahr oong mah•puh thoo meh•troo poor fuh•vaur
Which line for...?	**Qual é a linha para...?**
	kwahl eh uh lee•nyuh puh•ruh...
Do I have to transfer [change]?	**Tenho que mudar?** *teh•nyoo keh moo•dahr*
Is this the metro to...?	**Este trem vai para...?**
	ehst treng veye puh•ruh...
Where are we?	**Onde estamos?**
	aund ee•stuh•mooz

For Tickets, see page 20.

São Paulo, Rio de Janeiro, Belo Horizonte, Porto Alegre and Recife have excellent modern metro systems, though not covering the whole city. Tickets available are: **unitário** (one-way), **múltiplo 2** (round-trip), **múltiplo 10** (ten trips) and **integração** (one metro + one bus).

Boat & Ferry

When is the ferry to…?	**Quando é a balsa para…?** _kwuhn·doo eh uh bahl·suh puh·ruh…_
Can I take my car?	**Posso levar o meu carro?** _paw·soo loo·vahr oo mehoo kah·rroo_
What time is the next sailing?	**A que horas parte o próximo barco?** _au qeh aw·ruhz pahr·teh oo praw·see·moo bahr·koo_
Can I book a seat/cabin?	**Posso reservar um lugar/uma cabine?** _paw·soo reh·zehr·vuhr oong loo·gahr/oo·muh kuh·bee·nuh_
How long is the crossing?	**Quanto tempo demora a viagem?** _kwuhn·too tehm·poo deh·maw·ruh uh vee·ah·zseng_

There are specially organized cruises in all coastal towns in Brazil for visits to main beaches and nearby islands. Transport between Belém, Manaus and Santarém can be done by boat across the Amazon River, departing from **hidroviárias** (ferry terminals); for the long night journey, a hammock on deck is preferable to a hot cabin. Cruises on the Amazon are run by the state-owned **Empresa de Navegação da Amazônia (E.N.A.S.A.)** and a number of private companies.

YOU MAY SEE...

BARCO SALVA-VIDAS	life boat
COLETE SALVA-VIDAS	life jacket

Taxi

Where can I get a taxi?	**Onde posso pegar um táxi?** *aund paw•soo peh•gahr oong tahk•see*
Can you send a taxi?	**Pode enviar um táxi?** *pawd ehn•vee•ahr oong tahk•see*

I'd like a taxi now/ for tomorrow at…	**Queria um táxi agora/amanhã às…** *keh·ree·uh oong tahk·see uh·gaw·ruh/uh·muh·nyuh ahz…*
Pick me up at… (place/time)	**Me pegue no/às…** *meh peh·geh noo/ahz…*
I'm going to…	**Vou para…** *vau·oo puh·ruh…*
this address	**este endereço** *ehst ehn·deh·reh·soo*
the airport	**o aeroporto** *oo uh·eh·rau·paur·too*
the train [railway] station	**à estação dee trem** *ah ee·stuh·sohm deh treng*
I'm late.	**Estou atrasado *m* /atrasada *f*.** *ee·stawoo uh·truh·zah·thoo/uh·truh·zah·thuh*
Can you drive faster/ slower?	**Pode dirigir mais rápido/devagar?** *pawd dee·ree·jeer meyez rrah·pee·thoo/deh·vuh·gahr*
Stop/Wait here.	**Pare/Espere aqui.** *pah·reh/ee·speh·reh uh·kee*
How much?	**Quanto é?** *kwuhn·too eh*
You said it would cost…reais.	**Disse que ia custar…reais.** *thee·seh keh ee·uh koo·stahr…rree·eyez*
A receipt, please.	**Um recibo, por favor.** *oong reh·see·boo por fahz fuh·vaur*
Keep the change.	**Guarde o troco.** *goo·ahr·deh oo trau·koo*

YOU MAY HEAR…

Para onde? *puh·ruh aun·deh*	Where to?
Qual é o endereço? *kwahl eh uh ehn·deh·reh·soo*	What's the address?
Há uma taxa extra noturna/de aeroporto. *ah oo·muh tah·shuh ehs·truh naw·toor·nuh/ deh uh·eh·rau·paur·too*	There's a nighttime/ airport surcharge.

Taxis are yellow in Rio de Janeiro and white in São Paulo. Fares
are generally cheap. All Brazilian taxis have meters, except in
small towns, where the fare should be agreed in advance.
R\$ 0.20–0.90 is an approriate tip.

Bicycle & Motorbike

Where can I rent...?	**Onde posso alugar...?** *aund <u>paw</u>•soo uh•loo•<u>gahr</u>...*	
a 3-/10-speed bicycle	**uma bicicleta de trêz/dez velocidades [marchas]** *<u>oo</u>•muh bee•see•<u>kleh</u>•tuh deh trehz/dehz veh•<u>law</u>•see•<u>dah</u>•dehz [<u>mahr</u>•shuhz]*	
a moped	**uma lambreta** *<u>oo</u>•muh luhm•<u>breh</u>•tuh*	
a motorcycle	**uma motocicleta** *<u>oo</u>•muh maw•taw•see•<u>kleh</u>•tuh*	
How much per day/week?	**Quanto custa por dia/semana?** *<u>kwuhn</u>•too <u>koo</u>•stuh poor <u>dee</u>•uh/seh•<u>muh</u>•nuh*	
Can I have a helmet/lock?	**Posso ter uma capacete/corrente?** *<u>paw</u>•soo tehr <u>oo</u>•muh kuh•puh•<u>seh</u>•the/koo•<u>rrehnt</u>*	

Car Hire

Where can I rent a car?	**Onde posso alugar um carro?** *aund <u>paw</u>•soo uh•loo•<u>gahr</u> oong <u>kah</u>•rroo*
I'd like to rent...	**Queria alugar...** *keh•<u>ree</u>•uh uh•loo•<u>gahr</u>...*
a cheap/small car	**um carro barato/pequeno** *oong <u>kah</u>•rroo buh•rah•too/peh•keh•noo*
a 2-/4-door car	**um carro de duas/quatro portas** *oong <u>kah</u>•rroo deh <u>thoo</u>•uhz/<u>kwah</u>•troo <u>pawr</u>•tuhz*
a(n) automatic/manual	**um carro automático/manual** *oong <u>kah</u>•rroo awoo•too•<u>mah</u>•tee•koo/mah.noo.ahl*
a car with air conditioning	**um carro com ar condicionado** *oong <u>kah</u>•rroo kaum ahr kawn•<u>dee</u>•seeoo•<u>nah</u>•thoo*

a car seat	**um assento de carro de bebê** *oong uh•<u>sehn</u>•too deh <u>kah</u>•rroo deh beh•<u>beh</u>*
How much…	**Quanto é…?** *<u>kwuhn</u>•too eh…*
per day/week	**por dia/semana** *poor <u>dee</u>•uh/seh•<u>muh</u>•nuh*
per kilometer	**por quilômetro** *poor kee•<u>law</u>•meh•troo*
for unlimited mileage	**com quilometragem ilimitada** *kaum kee•lae•meh•<u>trah</u>•zseng ee•lee•mee•<u>tah</u>•thuh*
with insurance	**com seguro** *kaum seh•<u>goo</u>•roo*
Are there any discounts?	**Há descontos?** *ah dehs•<u>kaum</u>•tooz*

Fuel Station

Where's the next fuel station?	**Onde é o posto mais próximo?** *aund eh oo <u>paws</u>•too meyez <u>praw</u>•see•moo*
Fill it up, please.	**Encha o tanque, por favor.** *<u>ehn</u>•shuh oo <u>tuhn</u>•keh poor fuh•<u>vaur</u>*
…liters, please.	**…litros, por favor.** *…<u>lee</u>•trooz poor fuh•<u>vaur</u>*
I'll pay in cash/by credit card.	**Pago com dinheiro/com o cartão de crédito.** *<u>pah</u>•goo kaum dee•<u>nyay</u>•roo/kaum oo kuhr•<u>tohm</u> deh <u>kreh</u>•dee•too*

YOU MAY HEAR...

Tem uma carta de condução internacional? Do you have an
teng oo·muh kahr·tuh deh kaum·doo·sohm international driver's
een·tehr·nuh·see·oo·nahl license?

O seu passaporte, por favor. *oo sehoo* Your passport, please.
pah·suh·pawr·teh poor fuh·vaur

Quer seguro? *kehr seh·goo·roo* Do you want insurance?

É preciso deixar um sinal de... There is a deposit of...
eh preh·see·zoo day·shahr oong see·nahl deh...

Assine aqui, por favor. *uh·see·neh uh·kee* Please sign here.
poor fuh·vaur

YOU MAY SEE...

NORMAL	regular
SUPER	premium [super]
DIESEL	diesel

Asking Directions

Is this the right road to...?	**Esta é a estrada que vai para...?** *eh·stuh eh uh ee·strah·duh keh veye puh·ruh...*
How far is it to...?	**A que distância fica...?** *uh keh dee·stuhn·see·uh fee·kuh...*
Where's...?	**Onde fica...?** *aund fee·kuh...*
...Street	**a rua...** *uh rroo·uh...*
this address	**neste endereço** *nehst ehn·deh·reh·soo*
the highway [motorway]	**a estrada** *uh strah·duh*

| Can you show me on the map? | **Pode indicar no mapa?** *pawd een·dee·kahr noo mah·puh* |
| I'm lost. | **Estou perdido** *m* **/perdida** *f.* *ee·stawoo pehr·dee·doo/pehr·dee·duh* |

Parking

Can I park here?	**Posso estacionar aqui?** *paw·soo ee·stuh·seeoo·nahr uh·kee*
Where is the nearest parking garage/ parking lot [car park]?	**Onde fica a garagem mais próxima/o estacionamento mais próximo?** *aund fee·kuh uh guh·rah·zseng meyez praw·see·muh/ oo ee·stuh·seeawn·uh·mehn·too meyez praw·see·moo*
Where's the parking meter?	**Onde está o parquímetro?** *aund ee·stah oo pahr·kee·meh·troo*

YOU MAY HEAR...

sempre em frente *sehm·preh eng frehn·teh*	straight ahead
à esquerda *ah ee·skehr·duh*	on the left
à direita *ah dee·ray·tuh*	on the right
depois da/ao dobrar a esquina *deh·poyz dah/ahoo doo·brahr uh ees·kee·nuh*	on/around the corner
em frente de *eng frehn·teh deh*	opposite
por trás de *poor trahz deh*	behind
a seguir ao *m* **/à** *f* *uh seh·geer ahoo/ah*	next to
depois do *m* **/da** *f* *deh·poyz thoo/duh*	after
norte/sul *nawrt/sool*	north/south
leste/oeste *lehs·the/aw·ehs·teh*	east/west
no semáforo *noo seh·mah·fau·roo*	at the traffic light
no cruzamento *noo croo·zuh·mehn·too*	at the intersection

YOU MAY SEE...

	proibido ultrapassar	do not pass
	sentido proibido	no entry
	estacionamento proibido	no parking
(50)	**limite de velocidade**	speed limit
STOP	**parada obrigatória**	stop
	final de faixa	lane ends
	dar prioridade	yield

How much?   **Quanto é...?** _kwuhn•too eh..._
  per hour   **por hora** _poor aw•ruh_
  per day   **por dia** _poor dee•uh_
  overnight   **só uma noite** _saw oo•muh noyt_

Parking can be difficult in big cities. Always lock your car and
never leave anything in sight (even if you consider it not valuable)
as it can encourage break-ins. Parking "guards" tend to appear within
seconds of parking your car, offering to watch over it for you for a
(modest) fee. It is advisable to agree to this as otherwise you may risk
returning to a slightly damaged vehicle. Licensed guards operate in Rio
and São Paulo. They will issue a receipt that covers a set period of time.

Rio drivers are especially notorious for their erratic lane-changing, in-town speeding and disregard for pedestrians and other drivers on the road. Be on the defensive and expect the unexpected. Speeding fines can be huge (several hundred dollars) even if going only slightly over the limit, which can change erratically. Be warned, it is polite to beep your horn when overtaking, and flashing your lights as a warning is common. It is illegal to drink and drive and there is a zero tolerance policy in operation. If in doubt, take a cab.

Breakdown & Repair

My car broke down/ won't start.	**O meu carro quebrou/O motor não pega.** *oo mehoo kah•rroo keh•brawoo/oo moo•taur nohm peh•guh*
Can you fix it (today)?	**Pode consertá-lo (hoje)?** *pawd kaum•sehr•tah•loo (oyzseh)*
When will it be ready?	**Quando estará pronto?** *kwuhn•doo ee•stuh•rah praun•too*
How much is it?	**Quanto custa?** *kwuhn•too koo•stuh*
I have a puncture/flat tyre (tire).	**Tenho um furo/pneu sem ar.** *teh•nyoo oong foo•roo/pnehoo seng ahr*

Accidents

There has been an accident.	**Houve um acidente.** *auoov oong uh•see•dehnt*
Call an ambulance/ the police.	**Chame uma ambulância/a polícia.** *shuh•meh oo•muh uhm•boo•luhn•see•uh/uh poo•lee•see•uh*

Places to Stay

ESSENTIAL

Can you recommend a hotel?	**Pode recomendar um hotel?** *pawd reh•kaw•mehn•dahr oong aw•tehl*
I have a reservation.	**Tenho uma reserva.** *teh•nyoo oo•muh reh•zehr•vuh*
My name is…	**Meu nome é…** *mehoo naum•eh eh…*
Do you have a room…?	**Tem um quarto…?** *teng oong kwahr•too…*
for one/two	**para um/dois** *puh•ruh oong/doyz*
with a bathroom	**com banheiro** *kaum buh•nyay•roo*
with air conditioning	**com ar condicionado** *kaum ar kawn•dee•seeoo•nah•thoo*
For…	**Para…** *puh•ruh…*
tonight	**hoje à noite** *auzseh ah noyt*
two nights	**duas noites** *thoo•uhz noytz*
one week	**uma semana** *oo•muh seh•muh•nuh*
How much is it?	**Quanto custa?** *kwuhn•too koo•stuh*
Do you have anything cheaper?	**Há mais barato?** *ah meyez buh•rah•too*
What time is check-out?	**A que horas temos de deixar o quarto?** *uh kee aw•ruhz teh•mooz deh thay•shahr oo kwahr•too*
Can I leave this in the safe?	**Posso deixar isto no cofre?** *paw•soo thay•shahr ee•stoo noo kaw•freh*
Can I leave my bags?	**Posso deixar a minha bagagem?** *paw•soo day•shahr uh mee•nyuh buh•gah•geng*
Can I have the bill/ a receipt?	**Pode me dar a conta/um recibo?** *pawd meh dahr uh kaum•tuh/oong reh•see•boo*
I'll pay in cash/by credit card.	**Pago com dinheiro/com o cartão de crédito.** *pah•goo kaum dee•nyay•roo/kaum oo kuhr•tohm deh kreh•dee•too*

Somewhere to Stay

Can you recommend…?	**Pode recomendar…?** *pawd reh•kaw•mehn•dahr*
a hotel	**um hotel** *oong aw•tehl*
a hostel	**um albergue** *oong ahl•behrg*
a campsite	**um parque de campismo** *oong pahr•keh deh kuhm•peez•moo*
a bed and breakfast	**uma pousada** *oo•muh pawoo•zah•thuh*
What is it near?	**É perto de quê?** *eh pehr•too deh keh*
How do I get there?	**Como se vai para lá?** *kau•moo seh veye puh•ruh lah*

At the Hotel

I have a reservation.	**Tenho uma reserva.** *teh•nyoo oo•muh reh•zehr•vuh*
My name is…	**Meu nome é…** *mehoo naum•ee eh…*
Do you have a room…?	**Tem um quarto…?** *teng oong kwahr•too…*
with a bathroom [toilet]/shower	**com banheiro/chuveiro** *kaum buh•nyay•roo/shoo•vay•roo*
with air conditioning	**com ar condicionado** *kaum ar kawn•dee•seeoo•nah•thoo*
that's smoking/ non-smoking	**para fumantes/não-fumantes** *puh•ruh foo•muhnts/nohm-foo•muhnts*

For…	**Para…** _puh·ruh…_
tonight	**hoje à noite** _auzseh <u>ah</u> noyt_
two nights	**duas noites** _<u>thoo</u>·uhz noytz_
one week	**uma semana** _<u>oo</u>·muh seh·<u>muh</u>·nuh_
Does the hotel have…?	**O hotel tem…?**
	oo aw·<u>tehl</u> teng…
a computer	**um computador** _oong kaum·poo·tuh·<u>daur</u>_
an elevator [lift]	**um elevador** _oong eh·leh·<u>vuh</u>·daur_
(wireless) internet service	**serviço de internet (sem fios)** _sehr·<u>vee</u>·soo deh een·tehr·<u>neht</u> (seng fee·ooz)_
room service	**serviço de quartos**
	sehr·<u>vee</u>·soo deh <u>kwahr</u>·tooz
a pool	**piscina** _pee·<u>see</u>·nuh_
a gym	**uma academia**
	oo·muh ah·kah·duh·mee·ah
I need…	**Preciso de…** _preh·<u>see</u>·zoo deh…_
an extra bed	**outra cama** _<u>auoo</u>·truh <u>kuh</u>·muh_
a cot	**cama de lona** _<u>kuh</u>·muh deh <u>law</u>·nuh_
a crib	**uma cama de bebê**
	<u>oo</u>·muh <u>kuh</u>·muh de beh·<u>beh</u>

For Numbers, see page 173.

In Brazil, the cheapest place to stay is the **dormitório**, providing a shared room for a few **reais** per night. Other kinds of lodging include:

Hotel In Brazil, most hotels are regulated by **Embratur** (the Brazilian Tourism Authority). There are five official categories.

Hotel-Apartamento Apartment hotels ranging from 2- to 4-star.

Hotel fazenda Farmhouse lodges, generally equipped with a swimming pool, tennis court and horseback-riding facilities.

Pousada A state-owned inn converted from an old castle, monastery, convent, palace or in a location of interest to tourists.

Pensão Corresponds to a boarding house. Usually divided into four categories.

Pousada de juventude Youth hostel; there are over 90 youth hostels in Brazil, which are open to anyone, regardless of age, though members can obtain discounts. Hostels are extremely popular and the best ones book up quickly so it is best to book these in advance.

Residencial Bed and breakfast accommodations.

Price

How much per night/week?	**Quanto é por noite/semana?** _kwuhn•too eh poor noyt/seh•muh•nuh_
Does the price include breakfast/sales tax?	**O preço inclui o café da manhã/taxas?** _oo preh•soo een•kloo•ee oo kuh•feh duh muh•nyuh/tah•shuhz_
Are there any discounts?	**Há algum desconto?** _ah ahl•goong dehs•kaum•too_

Preferences

Can I see the room?	**Posso ver o quarto?** *paw·soo vehr oo kwahr·too*	
I'd like a...room.	**Queria um... quarto.** *keh·ree·uh oong...kwahr·too*	
better	**melhor** *meh·lyohr*	
bigger	**maior** *muh·eeohr*	
cheaper	**mais barato** *meyez buh·rah·too*	
quieter	**mais silencioso** *meyez see·lehn·see·aw·zoo*	
I'll take it.	**Fico com esse.** *fee·koo kaum eh·seh.*	
No, I won't take it.	**Não, não fico com esse.** *nohm, nohm fee·koo kaum eh·seh*	

Questions

Where's...?	**Onde é...?** *aund eh...*	
the bar	**o bar** *oo bar*	
the bathroom [toilet]	**a casa de banho [o banheiro]** *uh kah·zuh deh buh·nyoo [oo buh·nyay·roo]*	
the elevator [lift]	**o elevador** *oo eh·leh·vuh·daur*	
Can I have...?	**Queria um...** *keh·ree·uh oong...*	
a blanket	**um cobertor** *oong koo·behr·taur*	
an iron	**um ferro** *oong feh·rroo*	
a pillow	**um travesseiro** *oong truh·veh·say·roo*	

soap	**um sabonete** *oong suh·boo·neht*
toilet paper	**papel higiênico** *puh·pehl ee·zseh·nee·koo*
a towel	**uma toalha** *oo·muh too·ah·lyuh*
Do you have an adapter for this?	**Tem um adaptador para isto?** *teng oong uh·duhp·tuh·daur puh·ruh ee·stoo*
How do I turn on the lights?	**Como é que se acende as luzes?** *kau·moo eh keh seh uh·sehn·deh uhz loo·zehz*
Could you wake me at…?	**Podia acordar-me às…?** *poo·dee·uh uh·koor·dahr·meh ahz…*
Can I leave this in the safe?	**Posso deixar isto no cofre?** *paw·soo thay·shahr ee·stoo noo kaw·freh*
I'd like to get my things from the safe.	**Queria tirar as minhas coisas do cofre.** *keh·ree·uh tee·rahr uhz mee·nyuhz koy·zuhz thoo kaw·freh*
Is/Are there any mail/ messages for me?	**Há correio/alguma mensagem para mim?** *ah koo·rray·oo/ahl·goo·muh mehn·sah·zseng puh·ruh meeng*
Do you have a laundry service?	**Tem serviço de lavanderia?** *teng sehr·vee·soo deh luh·vuhn·deh·ree·uh*

Problems

There's a problem.	**Há um problema.** *ah oong proo·bleh·muh*
I've lost my key/ key card.	**Perdi a minha chave/carta de chave.** *pehr·dee uh mee·nyuh shahv/kahr·tuh deh shahv*
I've locked myself out of my room.	**Fechei-me fora do quarto.** *fee·shay·meh faw·ruh thoo kwahr·too*
There's no hot water/ toilet paper.	**Não há água quente/papel higiénico.** *nohm ah ah·gwuh kehnt/puh·pehl ee·zseh·nee·koo*
The room is dirty.	**O quarto está sujo.** *oo kwahr·too ee·stah soo·zsoo*
There are bugs in our room.	**Há insetos no quarto.** *ah een·seh·tooz noo kwahr·too*

...doesn't work.	**...tem um defeito.** ... *teng oong deh·fay·too*
Can you fix...?	**Pode arrumar...?** *pawd uh·rroo.mahr...*
the air conditioning	**o ar condicionado** *oo ar kawn·dee·seeoo·nah·thoo*
the fan	**o ventilador** *oo vehn·tee·luh·daur*
the heat [heating]	**o aquecimento** *oo uh·keh·see·mehn·too*
the lights	**as luzes** *uhz loo·zehz*
the TV	**a TV** *uh teh·veh*
the toilet	**o vaso sanitario** *oo vah·zoo suh·nee·tah·rio*
I'd like to move to another room.	**Queria mudar de quarto.** *keh·ree·uh moo·dahr deh kwahr·too*

YOU MAY SEE...

EMPURRAR/PUXAR	push/pull
O BANHEIRO/LAVABOS	bathroom/restroom [toilet]
CHUVEIRO	shower
ELEVADOR	elevator [lift]
ESCADAS	stairs
LAVANDERIA	laundry
NÃO PERTURBAR	do not disturb
PORTA DE INCÊNDIO	fire door
SAÍDA (DE EMERGÊNCIA)	(emergency) exit
CHAMADA PARA DESPERTAR	wake-up call

Public restrooms [toilets] can be found in shopping malls, hotels, restaurants, airports, bus stations, the better snack bars and gas stations. You won't find any in the street or in other public places, except for a few along Copacabana beach.

Checking Out

When's check-out?	**A que horas temos de deixar o quarto?** _uh kee aw•ruhz teh•mooz deh thay•shahr oo kwahr•too_
Could I leave my bags here until…?	**Posso deixar a minha bagagem aqui até…?** _paw•soo day•shahr uh mee•nyuh buh•gah•zseng uh•kee uh•teh…_
Can I have an itemized bill/a receipt?	**Pode me dar uma conta detalhada/ um recibo?** _pawd meh dahr oo•muh kaum•tuh deh•tuh•lyah•duh/oong reh•see•boo_
I think there's a mistake.	**Creio que se enganou.** _kray•oo keh seh ehn•guh•nau_
I'll pay in cash/by credit card.	**Pago com dinheiro/com o cartão de crédito.** _pah•goo kaum dee•nyay•roo/kaum oo kuhr•tohm deh kreh•dee•too_

Renting

I reserved an apartment/a room.	**Reservei um apartamento/quarto.** _reh•zehr•vay oong uh•puhr•tuh•mehn•too/ kwahr•too_
My name is…	**Meu nome é…** _mehoo naum•ee eh…_
Can I have the key/ key card?	**Posso ter a chave/carta de chave?** _paw•soo tehr uh shahv/kahr•tuh deh shahv_
Are there…?	**Tem…?** _teng…_

dishes	**a louça** *uh <u>lau</u>·suh*
pillows	**travesseiros** *truh·veh·<u>say</u>·roo*
sheets	**lençóis** *lehn·<u>soyz</u>*
towels	**toalhas** *too·<u>ah</u>·lyuhz*
utensils [cutlery]	**os talheres** *ooz tuh·<u>lyeh</u>·rehz*
When do I put out the bins/recycling?	**Quando ponho o lixo/o lixo para reciclar lá fora?** *<u>kwuhn</u>·doo <u>paw</u>·nyoo oo <u>lee</u>·shoo/ <u>lee</u>·shoo <u>puh</u>·ruh ree·see·<u>klahr</u> lah <u>faw</u>·ruh*
...is broken.	**...está quebrado m /quebrada f.** *...ee·<u>stah</u> keh·<u>brah</u>·doo/ keh·<u>brah</u>·duh*
How does...work?	**Como funciona...?** *<u>kau</u>·moo faun·see·<u>aw</u>·nuh...*
the air conditioner	**o ar condicionado** *oo ar kawn·dee·seeoo·<u>nah</u>·thoo*
the dishwasher	**a máquina de lavar pratos** *uh <u>mah</u>·kee·nuh deh luh·<u>vahr</u> <u>prah</u>·tooz*
the freezer	**o congelador** *oo kaum·zseh·luh·<u>daur</u>*
the heater	**o aquecedor** *oo uh·<u>keh</u>·seh·daur*
the microwave	**o microondas** *oo mee·krau·<u>aun</u>·duhz*
the refrigerator	**a geladeira** *uh zseh·luh·<u>thay</u>·ruh*
the stove	**o fogão** *oo foo·<u>gohm</u>*
the washing machine	**a máquina de lavar (roupa)** *uh <u>mah</u>·kee·nuh deh luh·<u>vahr</u> (<u>rauoo</u>·puh)*

Domestic Items

I need...	**Preciso de...** *preh·<u>see</u>·zoo deh...*
an adapter	**um adaptador** *oong uh·duhp·tuh·<u>daur</u>*
aluminum [kitchen] foil	**papel de alumínio** *puh·<u>pehl</u> deh uh·loo·<u>mee</u>·nee·oo*
a bottle opener	**um abridor de garrafas** *uh·bree·<u>daur</u> deh guh·<u>rrah</u>·fuhz*
a broom	**uma vassoura** *<u>oo</u>·muh vuh·<u>sau</u>·ruh*
a can opener	**um abridor de latas** *ah·bree·<u>daur</u> deh <u>lah</u>·tuhz*

A service charge is generally added to your hotel and restaurant bills. However, if the service has been particularly good, you may want to leave an extra tip. The following is a guide:

Bellman, per bag	R$ 5–10
Hotel maid	R$ 5–10
Restroom attendant	R$ 1–2

The electrical current in Brazil is not completely standardized. Some parts of Brazil are 220 V (Brasília, Florianópolis, Fortaleza, recife, and São Luís), while others, including Rio de Janeiro and São Paulo, are 110 V. Make sure to enquire about the voltage before you plug in any applicances and use an appropriate adaptor if necessary.

cleaning supplies	**produtos de limpeza**	prau·_thoo_·tooz deh leem·_peh_·zuh
a corkscrew	**um saca-rolhas**	oong sah·kuh·_rau_·lyuz
I need…	**Preciso de…**	preh·_see_·zoo deh…
detergent	**detergente em pó para a roupa**	deh·tehr·_zsehnt_ eng paw _puh_·ruh uh _rauoo_·puh
dishwashing liquid	**detergente para a louça**	deh·tehr·_zsehnt_ _puh_·ruh uh _lau_·suh
bin bags	**sacos para o lixo**	_sah_·kooz _puh_·ruh oo _lee_·shoo
a light bulb	**uma lâmpada elétrica**	_oo_·muh _luhm_·puh·duh ee·_leh_·tree·kuh
matches	**fósforos**	_fawz_·fuh·rooz
a mop	**o esfregão**	oo ees·fruh·_gohm_

paper napkins	**guardanapos de papel** *gwahr·duh·nah·pooz deh puh·pehl*
paper towels	**papel da cozinha** *puh·pehl duh koo·zee·nyuh*
plastic wrap [cling film]	**papel aderente** *puh·pehl uh·deh·rehnt*
a plunger	**um desentupidor** *oong deh·zehn·too·pee·daur*
scissors	**uma tesoura** *oo·muh teh·zau·ruh*
a vacuum cleaner	**um aspirador** *oong uh·spee·ruh·daur*

For In the Kitchen, see page 81.

At the Hostel

Do you have any places left for tonight?	**Ainda há vagas para hoje à noite?** *uh·een·duh ah vah·guhz puh·ruh auzeh ah noyt*
Can I have...?	**Queria...?** *keh·ree·uh...*
a single/double room	**um quarto individual/duplo** *oong kwahr·too een·dee·vee·doo·ahl/doo·ploo*
a blanket	**um cobertor** *oong koo·behr·taur*
a pillow	**um travesseiro** *oong truh·veh·say·roo*
sheets	**lençóis** *lehn·soyz*
a towel	**uma toalha** *oo·muh too·ah·lyuh*
Do you have lockers?	**Tem cacifos?** *teng kuh·see·fooz*
What time are the doors locked?	**A que horas fecham as portas?** *uh keh aw·ruhz feh·shohm uhz pawr·tuhz*

There are over 90 youth hostels (**albergues juveniles**) in Brazil. For a full list of establishments afiliated with Hostelling International, visit www. albergues.com.br.
Hostels are especially popular with backpackers and those traveling on a budget so it is advisable to book well in advance. Many can be found in great beach-side locations.

Do I need a membership card?	**Preciso de cartão de sócio?** *preh•see•zoo deh kuhr•tohm deh saw•see•oo*
Here's my international student card.	**Aqui está o meu cartão internacional de estudante.** *uh•kee ee•stah oo mehoo kuhr•tohm een•tehr•nuh•seeoo•nahl de ee•stoo•duhnt*

Going Camping

Can I camp here?	**Posso acampar aqui?** *paw•soo uh•kuhm•pahr uh•kee*
Where's the campsite?	**Onde é o parque de campismo [camping]?** *aund eh oo pahr•keh deh kuhm•peez•moo [kuhm•peeng]*
What is the charge per day/week?	**Qual é a tarifa por dia/semana?** *kwahl eh uh tuh•ree•fuh poor dee•uh/seh•muh•nuh*
Are there…?	**Há…?** *ah…*
cooking facilities	**uma área para se cozinhar** *oo•muh ah•ree•uh puh•ruh seh koo•zee•nyahr*
electrical outlets	**electricidade** *ee•leh•tree•see•dahd*
laundry facilities	**uma lavanderia** *oo•muh luh•vuhn•deh•ree•uh*
Are there…?	**Tem…?** *teng…*
showers	**um chuveiro** *oong shoo•vay•roo*
tents for rent [hire]	**barracas para alugue** *bah•hah•kaz puh•ruh uh•loo•gehr*
Where can I empty the chemical toilet?	**Onde posso esvaziar o banheiro químico?** *aund paw•soo ees•vee•ahr oo buh•nyay•roo kee•mee•koo*

YOU MAY SEE…

ÁGUA POTÁVEL	drinking water
É PROIBIDO ACAMPAR	no camping
É PROIBIDO ACENDER FOGOS/ CHURRASQUEIRAS	no fires/barbecues

Communications

ESSENTIAL

Where's an internet café?	**Onde fica um internet café?** *aund fee•kuh oong een•tehr•neht kuh•feh*
Can I access the Internet here?	**Tenho acesso à internet aqui?** *teh•nyoo uh•seh•soo ah een•tehr•neht uh•kee*
Can I check email here?	**Posso ler o meu e-mail aqui?** *paw•soo lehr oo mehoo ee•mehl uh•khee*
How much per (half) hour?	**Quanto é por (meia) hora?** *kwuhn•too eh poor (may•uh) aw•ruh*
How do I connect/ log on?	**Como conecto/faço o logon?** *kau•moo koo•nehk•too/fah•soo oo law•gawn*
A phone card, please.	**Um cartão telefónico, por favor.** *oong kuhr•tohm tehl•eh•fawn•ee•koo poor fuh•vaur*
Can I have your phone number?	**Pode me dar o seu número de telefone?** *pawd meh dahr oo sehoo noo•meh•roo deh tehl•fawn*
Here's my number/ email address.	**Este é o meu número/e-mail.** *ehst eh oo mehoo noo•meh•roo/ee•mehl*
Call me.	**Telefone-me.** *tehl•fawn•eh•meh*
Email me.	**Envie um e-mail.** *ehn•vee•eh oong ee•mehl*
Hello. This is…	**Alô. Meu nome é…** *aw•lah. Mehoo naum•eh eh…*
I'd like to speak to…	**Queria falar com…** *keh•ree•uh fuh•lahr kaum…*
Could you repeat that, please?	**Poderia repetir, por favor?** *poh•deh•ree•ah reh•peh•teer poor fuh•vaur*
I'll call back later.	**Chamo mais tarde.** *shuh•moo meyez tahr•deh*
Bye.	**Tchau.** *Cha•oo*
Where's the post office?	**Onde são os correios?** *aund sohm ooz koo•rray•ooz*
I'd like to send this to…	**Gostaria de mandar isto para…** *goo•stuh•ree•uh deh muhn•dahr ee•stoo puh•ruh…*

Online

Where's an internet café?	**Onde fica um internet café?** *aund fee-kuh oong een-tehr-neht kuh-feh*
Does it have wireless internet?	**Tem internet wireless?** *teng een-tehr-neht wire-less*
What is the WiFi password?	**Qual é a senha do WiFi?** *kwahl eh uh seh-nyuh doo WiFi*
Is the WiFi free?	**O WiFi é grátis?** *oo WiFi eh grah-teez*
Do you have bluetooth?	**Tem bluetooth?** *teng bluetooth*
How do I turn the computer on/off?	**Como ligo/desligo o computador?** *kau-moo lee-goo/dehz-lee-goo oo kaum-poo-tuh-daur*
Can I...?	**Posso...?** *paw-soo...*
access the internet	**acessar a internet** *uh-seh-ssahr uh een-tehr-neht*
check email	**ler o meu e-mail** *lehr oo mehoo ee-mehl*
print	**imprimir** *eeng-pree-meer*
How much per (half) hour?	**Quanto é por (meia) hora?** *kwuhn-too eh poor (may-uh) aw-ruh*
How do I...?	**Como...?** *kau-moo...*
connect/disconnect	**conecto/desconecto** *koo-nehk-too/dehz-koo-nehk-too*
log on/off	**faço o logon/logoff** *fah-soo oo law-gawn/law-gawf*
type this symbol	**digito este símbolo** *dee-gee-too ehst seem-boo-loo*
What's your email?	**Qual é o seu e-mail?** *kwahl eh oo sehoo ee-mehl*
My email is...	**O meu e-mail é...** *oo mehoo ee-mehl eh...*
Do you have a scanner?	**Tem um scanner?** *teng oong scanner*

Social Media

Are you on Facebook/Twitter?	**Está no Facebook/Twitter?** *ee·stah noo facebook/twitter*
What's your username?	**Qual é o seu nome de usuário?** *kwahl eh oo sehoo <u>naum</u>·eh deh <u>oo</u>· zuh·ah·<u>ree</u>·uh*
I'll add you as a friend.	**Vou adicioná-lo como amigo.** *vawoo·oo uh·dee·seeoo·<u>nah</u>·loo kau·<u>moo</u> uh·<u>mee</u>·goo*
I'll follow you on Twitter.	**Vou segui-lo no Twitter.** *vawoo·oo seh·<u>gee</u>·loo noo Twitter*
Are you following...?	**Está seguindo...?** *ee·stah uh seh·<u>gheeng</u>·doo...*
I'll put the pictures on Facebook/Twitter.	**Vou colocar as fotos no Facebook/Twitter.** *vawoo koo·<u>loo</u>·khahr uhz faw·tawz noo Facebook/Twitter*
I'll tag you in the pictures.	**Vou te marcar nas fotos.** *vawoo tee·mahr·<u>kahr</u> nuhz faw·<u>tawz</u>*

Phone

A phone card/prepaid phone, please.	**Um cartão de telefone pré-pago, por favor** *oong <u>kuhr</u>·tohm deh tehl·<u>fawn</u> preh·<u>pah</u>·goo poor fuh·<u>vaur</u>*
How much?	**Quanto é?** *<u>kwuhn</u>·too eh*
Where's the pay phone?	**Onde está o telefone pago?** *aund ee·stah oo tehl·fawn pah·goo*
My phone doesn't work here.	**O meu telefone não funciona aqui.** *oo meehoo tehl·<u>fawn</u> nohm foon·<u>seeaw</u>·nuh uh·<u>kee</u>*
What network are you on?	**Em que rede está?** *eng keh rreh·deh ee·stah*
Is it 3G?	**É 3G?** *eh trehz zseh*
I have run out of credit/minutes.	**Fiquei sem crédito/minutos.** *fee·<u>kay</u> seng kreh·<u>dee</u>·too/mee·<u>noo</u>·tooz*
Can I buy some credit?	**Posso comprar algum crédito?** *paw·soo kaum·prahr ahl·<u>goong</u> kreh·<u>dee</u>·too?*

YOU MAY SEE...

FECHAR	close
APAGAR	delete
E-MAIL	e-mail
SAÍDA	exit
AJUDA	help
MESSENGER	instant messenger
INTERNET	internet
LOGIN	login
(NOVA) MENSAGEM	(new) message
LIGADO/DESLIGADO	on/off
ABRIR	open
IMPRIMIR	print
GUARDAR	save
ENVIAR	send
NOME DO USUÁRIO/SENHA	username/password
INTERNET WIRELESS	wireless internet

Do you have a phone charger?
Tem um carregador de telefone? *teng oong kah•rreh•guh•daur deh tehl•fawn*

What's the area/ country code for...?
Qual é o código de área/país para...? *kwahl eh oo kaw•dee•goo deh ah•eh•ree•uh/puh•eez puh•ruh...*

What's the number for Information?
Qual é o número das Informações? *kwahl eh oo noo•meh•roo duhz eeng•foor•muh•soingz*

I'd like the number for...
Queria o número para... *keh•ree•uh oo noo•meh•roo puh•ruh...*

I'd like to call collect [reverse the charges].
Queria telefonar a cobrar no destino. *keh•ree•uh tehl•fawn•ahr uh koo•brahr noo dehz•tee•noo*

Can I have your number?
Pode me dar o seu número de telefone? *pawd meh dahr oo sehoo noo•meh•roo deh tehl•fawn*

Here's my number.	**Este é o meu número.** *ehst eh oo mehoo noo•meh•roo*
Call me.	**Me liga.** *meh lee•gah*
Text me.	**Mande uma mensagem de texto.** *muhn•duh oo•muh mehn•sah•zseng deh tehk•stoo*
I'll call you.	**Eu ligo.** *eeoo lee•guh*
I'll text you.	**Mando uma mensagem de texto.** *muhn•doo oo•muh mehn•sah•zseng deh tehk•stoo*

For Numbers, see page 173.

Telephone Etiquette

Hello. This is…	**Alô. Meu nome é…** *ah•lawoo. mehoo nau•mee eh…*
I'd like to speak to…	**Queria falar com…** *keh•ree•uh fuh•lahr kaum…*
Extension…	**Extensão…** *ehs•tehn•sohm…*
Speak louder/more slowly, please.	**Fale mais alto/devagar, por favor.** *fah•leh meyez ahl•too/deh•vuh•gahr poor fuh•vaur*
Could you repeat that?	**Poderia repetir?** *poh.deh.ree.ah reh•peh•teer*
I'll call back later.	**Eu ligo mais tarde.** *eeoo lee•guh meyez tahrd*
Bye.	**Tchau.** *Chah•oo*

For Business Travel, see page 147.

Payphones are easy to use but you will need to purchase a pre-paid calling card. You can buy these from any store displaying a sign reading **Cartão Telefônico Aqui**. Temporary mobile phones with 'pay as you go' plans are also available. The Brazilian internet market is huge and internet cafes can be found throughout the country, although connections in smaller beach resorts can be slow. Many larger hotels provide free WiFi.

YOU MAY HEAR...

Quem fala? *keng fah·luh*	Who's calling?
Não desligue. *nohm dehs·lee·geh*	Hold on.
Vou ligar agora. *vau lee·gahr uh·gaw·ruh*	I'll put you through.
Lamento, mas ele/ela não está. *luh·mehn·too muhz ehl/ehl·uh nohm ee·stah*	I'm afraid he's/she's not in.
Ele/Ela não pode atender o telefone. *ehl/ehl·uh nohm pawd uh·tehn·dehr oo tehl·fawn*	He/She can't come to the phone.
Quer deixar uma mensagem? *kehr day·shahr oo·muh mehn·sah·zseng*	Would you like to leave a message?
Ligue mais tarde/daqui dez minutos. *lee·geh meyez tahr·deh/da·kee·uh dehz mee·noo·tooz*	Call back later/in ten minutes.
Ele/Ela pode telefonar para você? *ehl/ehl·uh pawd tehl·fawn·ahr para voh·seh*	Can he/she call you back?
Qual é o seu número de telefone? *kwahl eh oo sehoo noo·meh·roo deh tehl·fawn*	What's your number?

Fax

Can I send/receive a fax here?	**Posso enviar/receber um fax aqui?** _paw·soo ehn·vee·ahr/reh·seh·behr oong fahks uh·kee_
What's the fax number?	**Qual é o número de fax?** _kwahl eh oo noo·meh·roo deh fahks_
Please fax this to...	**Por favor mande este fax para...** _poor fuh·vaur muhn·deh ehst fahks puh·ruh..._

Post

Where's the post office/mailbox [postbox]?	**Onde é que é o correio/a caixa do correio?** _aund eh keh eh oo koo·rray·oo/uh keye·shuh thoo koo·rray·oo_
A stamp for this postcard/letter, please.	**Um selo para este postal/esta carta, por favor.** _oong seh·loo puh·ruh ehst poo·stahl/eh·stuh kahr·tuh poor fuh·vaur_
How much?	**Quanto é?** _kwuhn·too eh_
I want to send this package by airmail/express.	**Queria mandar este embrulho por via aérea/correio expresso.** _keh·ree·uh muhn·dahr eh·stuh ehm·broo·lyoo poor vee·uh uh·eh·ree·uh/koo·rray·oo ees·preh·soo_
A receipt, please.	**Um recibo, por favor.** _oong reh·see·boo poor fuh·vaur_

Post offices bear the sign ECT (**Empresa de Correios e Telégrafos**) or a sign reading **Correios**; they are generally open from 9:00 a.m. to 5:00 p.m., Mondays through Fridays, and until 1:00p.m. on Saturdays. Street corner mailboxes are yellow.

YOU MAY HEAR...

**Por favor preencha a declaração da
alfândega.** *poor fuh•vaur pree•ehn•shuh uh
deh•kluh•ruh•sohm duh uhl•fuhn•dee•guh*

Qual é o valor? *kwahl eh oo vuh•laur*

O que é que tem dentro? *oo kee eh keh teng
dehn•troo*

Please fill out the customs
declaration form.

What's the value?

What's inside?

Food & Drink

Eating Out

ESSENTIAL

Can you recommend a good restaurant/bar?	**Pode recomendar um bom restaurante/bar?** *pawd reh·kaw·mehn·dahr oong bohng reh·stahoo·ruhnt/bar*
Is there a(n) traditional/ inexpensive restaurant near here?	**Há um restaurante tradicional/ barato perto daqui?** *ah oong reh·stuhoo·ruhnt truh·dee·see·oo·nahl/buh·rah·too pehr·too duh·kee*
A table for…, please.	**Uma mesa para…, por favor.** *oo·muh meh·zuh puh·ruh…poor fuh·vaur*
Could we sit…?	**Podemos sentar…?** *poo·deh·mooz sehn·tahr…*
here/there	**aqui/ali** *uh·kee/uh·lee*
outside	**lá fora** *lah faw·ruh*
in a non-smoking area	**na área para não-fumantes** *nuh ah·ree·uh puh·ruh noh·foo·muhnts*
I'm waiting for someone.	**Estou à espera de alguém.** *ee·stawoo ah ee·speh·ruh deh ahl·gehm*
Where's the restroom [toilet]?	**Onde são os banheiros?** *aund sohm ooz buh·nyay·rooz*
A menu, please.	**Uma cardápio, por favor.** *oong car·dah·pee·oo poor fuh·vaur*
What do you recommend?	**O que é que me recomenda?** *oo keh eh keh meh reh·koo·mehn·duh*
I'd like…	**Queria…** *keh·ree·uh…*
Some more…, please.	**Mais…, por favor.** *meyez…poor fuh·vaur*
Enjoy your meal.	**Bom apetite.** *bohng uh·peh·tee·teh*
The check [bill], please.	**A conta, por favor.** *uh kaum·tuh poor fuh·vaur*

Is service included?	**O serviço está incluído?** *oo sehr•vee•soo ee•stah een•kloo•ee•thoo*
Can I pay by credit card?	**Posso pagar com cartão de crédito?** *paw•soo puh•gahr kaum kuhr•tohm deh kreh•dee•too*
Could I have a receipt, please?	**Pode me dar um recibo, por favor?** *pawd meh dahr oong reh•see•boo poor fuh•vaur*
Thank you.	**Obrigado** *m* **/Obrigada** *f.* *aw•bree•gah•thoo/aw•bree•gah•thuh*

Where to Eat

Can you recommend...?	**Pode recomendar...?** *pawd reh•koo•mehn•dahr...*
a restaurant	**um restaurante** *oong reh•stuhoo•ruhnt*
a bar	**um bar** *oong bar*
a cafe	**um café** *oong kuh•feh*
a fast-food place	**um restaurante de comida rápida [uma rede de fast food]** *oong reh•stuhoo•ruhnt deh koo•mee•duh rah•pee•duh [oo•muh rehd deh fast food]*
a seafood restaurant	**um restaurante de frutos do mar** *oong reh•stuhoo•ruhnt deh froo•tooz doo mahr*
a cheap restaurant	**um restaurante barato** *oong rehz•tahoo•ruhnt buh•rah•too*

an expensive resturant	**um restaurante caro** *oong rehz·tahoo·ruhnt kah·roo*	
a restaurant with a good view	**um restaurante com boa vista** *oong rehz·tahoo·ruhnt kaum bau·uh vee·stuh*	
an authentic/non-touristy restaurant	**um restaurante típico/não turístico** *oong rehz·tahoo·ruhnt tee·pee·koo/nohm too·ree·stee·koo*	

Reservations & Preferences

I'd like to reserve a table...	**Queria reservar uma mesa...** *keh·ree·uh reh·zehr·vahr oo·muh meh·zuh...*
for two	**para dois** *puh·ruh doyz*
for this evening	**para hoje à noite** *puh·ruh auzseh ah noyt*
for tomorrow at...	**para amanhã às...** *puh·ruh uh·muh·nyuh ahz...*
A table for two.	**Uma mesa para dois.** *oo·muh meh·zuh puh·ruh doyz*
We have a reservation.	**Temos uma reserva.** *teh·mooz oo·muh reh·zehr·vuh*
My name is...	**Meu nome é...** *mehoo naum·ee eh...*
Could we sit...?	**Podemos sentar...?** *poo·deh·mooz sehn·tahr...*
here/there	**aqui/ali** *uh·kee/uh·lee*
outside	**lá fora** *lah faw·ruh*
in a non-smoking area	**na área para não-fumantes** *nuh ah·ree·uh puh·ruh noh-foo·muhnts*
by the window	**à janela** *ah zsuh·neh·luh*
in the shade	**à sombra** *ah sohng·bruh*
in the sun	**ao sol** *ahoo sawl*
Where are the restrooms [toilets]?	**Onde são os banheiros?** *aund sohmuhz ooz buh·nyay·rooz*

YOU MAY HEAR...

Tem reserva? *teng reh·sehr·vuh*	Do you have a reservation?
Quantas pessoas? *kwuhn·tuhz peh·sau·uhs*	How many?
Fumante ou não-fumante? *foo·muhnt aw nohmfoo·muhnt*	Smoking or non-smoking?
Deseja encomendar? *deh·zeh·zsuh ehn·caw·mehn·dahr*	Would you like to order?
O que deseja? *oo keh deh·zeh·zsuh*	What would you like?
Recomendo... *reh·koo·mehn·doo...*	I recommend...
Bom apetite. *bohng uh·peh·tee·teh*	Enjoy your meal.

How to Order

Excuse me!	**Por favor!** *poor fuh·vaur*
We're ready to order.	**Estamos prontos para encomendar.** *ee·stuh·mooz prawn·tooz puh·ruh eng·kau·mehn·dahr*
The wine list, please.	**A carta de vinhos, por favor.** *uh kahr·tuh deh vee·nyooz poor fuh·vaur*
I'd like...	**Queria...** *keh·ree·uh...*
a bottle of...	**uma garrafa...** *oo·muh guh·rrah·fuh...*
a carafe of...	**um jarro de...** *oom jah·rroo deh...*
a glass of...	**um copo de...** *oong kaw·poo deh...*
A menu, please.	**Um cardápio, por favor.** *oong car·dah·pee·oo poor fuh·vaur*
Do you have...?	**Tem...?** *teng...*
a menu in English	**um cardápio em Inglês** *oong car·dah·pee·oo eng een·glehz*

a fixed-price menu	**um cardápio, de preço-fixo** _oong car·dah·pee·oo deh preh·soo feek·soo_
a children's menu	**um cardápio de criança** _oong car·dah·pee·oo deh kree·uhn·suh_
What do you recommend?	**O que é que me recomenda?** _oo kee eh keh meh reh·koo·mehn·duh_
What's this?	**O que é isto?** _oo kee eh ee·stoo_
What's in it?	**Leva o quê?** _leh·vuh oo keh_
Is it spicy?	**É picante?** _eh pee·kuhnt_
I'd like…	**Queria…** _keh·ree·uh…_
More…, please.	**Mais…, por favor.** _meyez… poor fuh·vaur_
With/Without…	**Com/Sem…** _kaum/seng…_
I can't have…	**Não posso comer…** _nohm paw·soo koo·mehr…_
rare	**mal passado** _m_ /**passada** _f mahl puh·sah·thoo/ puh·sah·thuh_
medium	**meio passado** _m_ /**passada** _f may·oo puh·sah·thoo/ puh·sah·thuh_
well-done	**bem passado** _m_ /**passada** _f beng puh·sah·thoo/ puh·sah·thuh_
It's to go [take away].	**É para levar.** _eh puh·ruh leh·vahr_

YOU MAY SEE…

COUVERT	cover charge
PREÇO-FIXO	fixed-price
CARDÁPIO	menu
CARDÁPIO DO DIA	menu of the day
SERVIÇO (NÃO) INCLUÍDO	service (not) included
ESPECIAIS	specials

Cooking Methods

baked	**dourado** m **/dourada** f _dauoo·rah·doo/dauoo·rah·duh_
boiled	**cozido** m **/cozida** f _koo·zee·thoo/koo·zee·thuh_
braised	**estufado** m **/estufada** f _ee·stoo·fah·thoo/_ _ee·stoo·fah·thuh_
breaded	**empanado** m **/empanada** f _ehm·puh·nah·doo/ehm·puh·nah·dah_
creamed	**com natas** _kohng nah·tuhz_
diced	**aos cubos** _ahooz koo·booz_
filet of...	**filete de...** _fee·leht deh..._
fried	**frito** m **/frita** f _free·too/free·tuh_
grilled	**grelhado** m **/grelhada** f _gree·lyah·thoo/_ _gree·lyah·thuh_
poached	**escalfado** m **/escalfada** f _ees·kahl·fah·thoo/_ _ees·kahl·fah·thuh_
roasted	**assado** m **/assada** f _uh·sah·thoo/uh·sah·thuh_
sautéed	**salteado** m **/salteada** f _sahl·tee·ah·thoo/_ _sahl·tee·ah·thuh_
smoked	**defumado** m **/defumada** f _deh·foo·mah·doo/deh·foo·mah·duh_
steamed	**cozido** m **/cozida** f **a vapor** _koo·zee·thoo/_ _koo·zee·thuh uh vuh·paur_
stewed	**guisado** m **/guisada** f _gee·zah·thoo/gee·zah·thuh_
stuffed	**recheado** m **/recheada** f _reh·shee·ah·thoo/_ _reh·shee·ah·thuh_

Dietary Requirements

I am...	**Sou...** _sauoo..._
diabetic	**diabético** m **/diabética** f _dee·uh·beh·tee·koo/_ _dee·uh·beh·tee·kuh_

lactose intolerant	**intolerante à lactose** *een•tawl•eh•<u>ruhnt</u> ah <u>lahk</u>•tawz*
vegetarian	**vegetariano** *m* /**vegetariana** *f* *veh•zseh•tuh•ree•<u>uh</u>•noo/veh•zseh•tuh•ree•<u>uh</u>•nuh*
vegan	**vegetariano** *veh•geh•tuh•ree•uh•noo*
I'm allergic to...	**Sou alérgico** *m* /**alérgica** *f* **a...** *sauoo uh•<u>lehr</u>•gee•koo/uh•<u>lehr</u>•gee•kuh uh...*
I can't eat...	**Não posso comer...** *nohm <u>paw</u>•soo koo•<u>mehr</u>...*
dairy	**lacticínios** *lahk•tee•<u>see</u>•nee•ooz*
gluten	**glúten** *gloo•<u>tehn</u>*
nuts	**nozes** *<u>naw</u>•zehz*
pork	**carne de porco** *<u>kahrr</u>•neh deh <u>paur</u>•koo*
shellfish	**marisco** *muh•<u>ree</u>•skoo*
spicy foods	**comidas picantes** *koo•<u>mee</u>•duhz pee•<u>kuhnts</u>*
wheat	**trigo** *<u>tree</u>•goo*
Is it halal/kosher?	**É halal/kosher?** *eh uh•<u>lahl</u>/<u>kaw</u>•shehr*
Do you have...?	**Tem...?** *teng...*
skimmed milk	**leite magro** *layt mah•groo*
whole milk	**leite gordo** *layt goahr•doo*
soya milk	**leite de soja** *layt deh saw•zsuh*

The most traditional Brazilian dishes are inspired by Portuguese and African foods, along with the everyday staples: rice, beans and **farihna** (dried, ground cassava). Expect to find seafood, fish, fresh sushi, barbecued meat (**churrasco**), hearty Italian dishes and delicious salads. In many restuarants, portions are large enough to share, and this is acceptable in all but the smartest of places.

Dining with Children

Do you have children's portions?	**Tem porções para crianças?** teng poor•soings puh•ruh kree•uhn•suhz
A child's seat, please.	**Um assento de criança, por favor.** oong uh•sehn•too deh kree•uhn•suh poor fuh•vaur
Can I have a highchair/child's seat?	**Tem uma cadeira alta/cadeirinha de criança?** teng oo•muh kuh•day•ruh ahl•tuh/kuh•day•ree•nyuh deh kree•uhn•suh
Where can I feed/change the baby?	**Onde posso alimentar/trocar o bebê [neném]?** aund paw•soo uh•lee•mehn•tahr/traw•kahr oo beh•beh [neh•neh]
Can you warm this?	**Pode aquecer isto?** pawd uh•keh•sehr ee•stoo

For Traveling with Children, see page 150.

How to Complain

How much longer will our food be?	**Quanto tempo demora a nossa comida?** kwuhn•too tehm•poo deh•maw•ruh uh naw•suh koo•mee•thuh
We can't wait any longer.	**Não podemos esperar mais.** nohm poo•deh•mooz ee•speh•rahr meyez
We're leaving.	**Vamo embora.** vuh•moo ehm•baw•ruh

I didn't order this.	**Não encomendei isso.** nohm ehn·koo·mehn·_day_ ee·soo
I ordered...	**Encomendei...** ehn·koo·mehn·_day_...
I can't eat this.	**Não posso comer isto.** nohm paw·soo koo·_mehr_ ee·stoo
This is too...	**Isto está muito...** ee·stoo ee·_stah_ _mooee_·too...
cold/hot	**frio/quente** _free_·oo/kehnt
salty/spicy	**salgado/picante** sahl·_gah_·thoo/pee·_kuhnt_
tough/bland	**duro/insosso** _doo_·roo/een·_saw_·soo
This isn't clean/fresh.	**Isto não está limpo/fresco.** ee·stoo nohm ee·_stah_ _leem_·poo/frehs·koo

Paying

The check [bill], please.	**A conta, por favor.** uh _kaum_·tuh poor fuh·_vaur_
Separate checks [bills], please.	**Contas separadas, por favor.** _kaum_·tuhz seh·puh·_rah_·duhz poor fuh·_vaur_
It's all together.	**É tudo junto.** eh _too_·doo _zsoon_·too
Is service included?	**O serviço está incluído?** oo sehr·_vee_·soo ee·_stah_ een·kloo·_ee_·thoo
What's this amount for?	**De que é este valor?** deh keh eh _eh_·stuh vuh·_loahr_
I didn't have that.	**Eu não comi isso. Eu comi...** ehoo nohm koo·_mee_ ee·soo. ehoo koo·_mee_...
I had...	
Can I pay by credit card?	**Posso pagar com cartão de crédito?** _paw_·soo puh·_gahr_ kaum kuhr·_tohm_ deh _kreh_·dee·too
Can I have an itemized bill/a receipt?	**Pode me dar uma conta detalhada/ um recibo?** pawd meh _dahr_ oo·muh _kaum_·tuh deh·tuh·_lyah_·duh/oong reh·_see_·boo
That was a very good meal.	**Foi uma refeição excelente.** foy _oo_·muh reh·fay·_sohm_ eh·seh·_lehnt_
I've already paid.	**Já paguei.** zsah puh·_gay_

Meals & Cooking

O pequeno almoço
Breakfast is usually served from 7:00 to 10:00 a.m. It can include coffee, rolls, butter and jam, along with fresh fruit juice, fruit, toast and pastries.

O almoço
Lunch is the main meal of the day, served from 12:30 to 2:30 p.m. Shops are normally closed during these hours. In Brazilian resorts, lunch is often served without interruption from 12:30 until the evening. It generally includes soup or salad, fish or meat, and a dessert.

O jantar
Dinner is served from about 8:00 to 11:00 p.m. It typically includes soup, fish or meat, salad, bread, and fruit or a sweet for dessert. Coffee or espresso is almost always served at the end of the meal.

Breakfast

a água uh _ah_•gwuh	water
o bolinho oo bau•_lee_•nyoo	muffin
o café.../chá... oo kuh•_feh_.../shah...	coffee.../tea...
com açúcar kaum uh•_soo_•kuhr	with sugar
com adoçante artificial kaum uh•thoo•_suhnt_ uhr•tee•fee•see•_ahl_	with artificial sweetner
com leite kaum layt	with milk
descafeínado dehz•kuh•fay•_nah_•thoo	decaf
cafezinho kuh•feh•_zee_•nyoo	black
as carnes frias uhz _kahr_•nehz _free_•uhz	cold cuts [charcuterie]
o cereal (frio/quente) oo seh•ree•_ahl_ (_free_•oo/kehnt)	(cold/hot) cereal

a geleia *ah zseh•lay•uh*	jam
a farinha de aveia *uh fuh•ree•nyuh deh uh•vay•uh*	oatmeal
o leite *oo layt*	milk
a manteiga *uh muhn•tay•guh*	butter
a omelete *uh aw•meh•leh•tuh*	omelet
o iogurte *uh yaw•goort*	yogurt
o ovo... *oo au•voo...*	...egg
muito fervido/fervido macio *mooee•too fehr•vee•thoo/fehr•vee•thoo muh•see•oo*	hard-boiled/ soft-boiled
estrelado [frito] *ee•struh•lah•doo [free•too]*	fried
mexido *meh•shee•doo*	scrambled
o pão *oo pohm*	bread
o pãozinho *oo pohm•zee•nyoo*	roll
o queijo *oo kay•zsoo*	cheese
as salsichas *uhz sahl•see•shuhz*	sausages
o suco de... *oo soo•koo deh*	...juice
fruta *froo•tuh*	fruit
maçã *muh•suh*	apple
toranja *uh taw•ruhn•zsuh*	grapefruit
laranja *luh•ruhn•zsuh*	orange
o toucinho *oo taw•see•nyoo*	bacon
as torradas *uhz too•rrah•duhz*	toast
o jogurte *oo yaw•goort*	yogurt

Appetizers

as carnes frias *uhz kahr•nehz free•uhz*	cold cuts
o chouriço *oo shauoo•ree•soo*	sausage
as lulas à milanesa *uhz loo•luhz ah mee•luh•neh•zuh*	squid
o paio *oo peye•oo*	smoked pork fillet

os pimentões assados *ooz pee·mehn·toehnz uh·sah·dooz* — roasted peppers

o pipis *oo pee·peez* — spicy chicken stew

siri recheada *see·ree eh·shee·ah·thuh* — stuffed crab

Soup

o caldo verde *oo kahl·doo vehrd* — potato and kale soup with sausage

o gaspacho *oo guhz·pah·shoo* — chilled soup with tomatoes, sweet peppers, onions, cucumbers and croutons

a sopa de bacalhau *a sau·puh buh·kuh·lyahoo* — dried cod soup with garlic and bread

a sopa de pão *a sau·puh duh pohm* — bread soup with garlic and herbs

a sopa de carne com legumes e macarrão *a sau·puh deh kahrn kaum leh·goomz eh muh·kuh·rrohm* — meat broth with vegetables and macaroni

a sopa seca *uh sau·puh seh·kuh* — thick soup with meat, cabbage and bread

a sopa transmontana *a sau·puh truhnz·moo·tuh·nuh* — vegetable soup with bacon and bread

a sopa... *uh sau·puh...* — ...soup

   à pescador *ah pehs·kuh·daur* — fish

   canja *keng·zsuh* — chicken and rice

   de abóbora *deh uh·baw·buh·ruh* — pumpkin

   de agriões *deh uh·gree·oings* — potato and watercress

   de coentro *deh koo·eng·troo* — coriander, bread, and poached eggs

   de ervilha *deh eer·vee·lyuh* — green pea

Fish & Seafood

o atum *oo uh·toong* — tuna

as amêijoas à Bulhão Pato — clams with coriander, garlic
uhz uh·may·zsoo·uhz ah boo·lyohm pah·too — and onion

as amêijoas à Portuguesa — clams with garlic, parsley and
uhz uh·may·zsoo·uhz ah poor·too·geh·zuh — olive oil

o bacalhau à Gomes de Sá — dried cod with olives, garlic,
oo buh·kuh·lyahoo ah gau·mehz deh sah — onions, parsley and hard-
boiled eggs

o bacalhau podre *oo buh·kuh·lyahoo pau·dreh* — baked layers of cod and fried
potatoes

a cabeça de pescada cozida — fish stew
uh kuh·beh·suh deh peh·skah·thuh koo·zee·thuh

os camarões... *ooz kuh·muh·roings...* — ...shrimp [prawns]

   fritos *free·tooz* — fried

   grandes *gruhn·dehz* — large [king]

   no espeto *noo ee·speh·too* — on a stick

a caldeirada... *uh kahl·day·rah·thuh...* — fish with onions, tomatoes,
potatoes, olive oil...

   à fragateira *ah fruh·guh·tay·ruh* — shellfish and mussels in a fish
stock with tomatoes

A popular Portuguese import is **bacalhau** (dried, salted cod). On sale in shops and markets, it looks like sheets of stiff, gray cardboard, but when soaked and cooked it is transformed. It is regularly seen on menus as **bolinhos de bacalhau**, meltingly rich rissoles (croquettes). Also look out for **cozido**, another Portuguese dish made up of stewed meats and vegetables served with broth.

à moda da Póvoa *ah maw·duh duh praw·voo·uh*	hake, skate, sea bass and eel
o espadarte *oo ees·puh·dahrt*	swordfish
a lagosta *uh luh·gau·stuh*	lobster
a lampreia *uh luhm·pray·uh*	lamprey
o linguado *oo leeng·gwah·thoo*	sole
as lulas *uhz loo·luhz*	squid
as lulas recheadas *uhz loo·luhz reh·shee·ah·duhz*	stuffed squid
os mariscos *ooz muh·rees·kooz*	seafood
a moqueca de peixe *uh moo·keh·kuh deh paysh*	stew made of fish, shellfish or shrimp with coconut milk
as ostras *uhz aw·struhz*	oysters in butter and wine
o pargo *oo pahr·goo*	bream
o polvo *oo paul·voo*	octopus
o vatapá *oo vuh·tuh·pah*	fish and shrimp in a paste made of flour or breadcrumbs

Meat & Poultry

o arroz de frango *oo uh•rrauz deh fruhn•goo*
chicken with white wine, ham and rice

o bife [filé] *oo beef [fee•leh]*
steak

o bife na frigideira *oo beef nuh free•zsuh•day•ruh*
steak fried in butter, white wine and garlic

o carneiro *oo kuhr•nay•roo*
lamb

a carne de porco *uh kahrn deh paur•koo*
pork

a carne de sol com feijão verde *uh kahrn deh sol kaum fay•zsohm vehrd*
sun-dried meat (jerky) with green beans

a carne de vaca *uh kahrn deh vah•kuh*
beef

o carneiro guisado [ensopado] *oo kuhrr•nay•roo gee•zah•thoo [eng•soo•pah•do]*
mutton with tomatoes, garlic and herbs

o coelho *oo koo•eh•lyoo*
rabbit

a costeleta *uh koo•stuh•leh•tuh*
cutlet

o cozido à Portuguesa *oo koo•zee•doo ah poor•too•geh•zuh*
boiled beef, bacon, smoked sausage and vegetables

a feijoada *uh fay•zsoo•ah•duh*
Brazil's national dish: black beans cooked with bacon, salted pork, jerky and sausage

o frango *oo fruhn•goo*
chicken

o frango na púcara *oo fruhn•goo nuh poo•keh•ruh*
chicken stewed in port and cognac, then fried with almonds

o medalhão *uh meh•duh•lyohm*
tenderloin steak

a perdiz à caçador *oo pehr•deez uh kuh•suh•daur*
partridge simmered with carrots, onions, white wine and herbs

o presunto *oo preh•zoon•too*
cured ham

as tripas à moda do Porto *uhz tree·puhz ah maw·duh thoo paur·too* tripe cooked with pork, beans and chicken

a vitela *uh vee·tehl·uh* veal

o xinxim de galinha *oo sheeng·sheeng deh guh·lee·nyuh* chicken cooked in dried shrimp, peanuts and parsley

Vegetables & Staples

o açafrão *oo uh·suh·frohm* saffron

o acarajé *oo uh·kuh·ruh·zseh* grated beans fried in palm oil, served with pepper sauce, onions and shrimp

o açúcar *oo uh·soo·kuhr* sugar

as alcaparras *uhz ahl·kuh·pah·rruhz* capers

a alface *uh ahl·fah·seh* lettuce

as amêndoas *uhz uh·mehn·doo·uhz* almonds

o arroz... *oo uh·rrauz...* rice...

    de alhos *deh ah·lyooz* with garlic

    de cozido *deh koo·zee·thoo* cooked in meat stock

    de feijão *de fay·zsohm* with beans

as batatas... *uhz buh·tah·tuhz...* potatoes...

    cozidas *koo·zee·duhz* boiled

    cozidas com pele *koo·zee·duhz kohm pehl* boiled in their skins

    fritas *free·tuhz* fries [chips]

    de palha *deh pah·lyuh* matchsticks

o puré de batatas *oo poo·reh deh buh·tah·tuhz* mashed potatoes

as cebolas *uhz seh·bau·luhz* onions

os cogumelos *ooz koo·goo·meh·looz* mushrooms

as ervilhas *uhz eer·vee·lyuhz* peas

a farinha *uh fuh·ree·nyuh* flour

as favas *uhz fah·vuhz* broad beans

o feijão *oo fay·zsohm* kidney beans

o feijão verde *oo fay·<u>zsohm</u> vehrd*	green beans
o manjericão *oo muhn·zseh·ree·<u>kohm</u>*	basil
a manteiga *uh muhn·<u>tay</u>·guh*	butter
as massas *uhz <u>mah</u>·suhz*	pasta
o pão *oo pohm*	bread
os pimentões *ooz pee·<u>mehn</u>·toehnz*	peppers
o rutu à mineira *oo rroo·<u>too</u> ah mee·<u>nay</u>·ruh*	beans, cassava, flour, pork, cabbage, fried eggs and bacon
a salsa *uh <u>sahl</u>·suh*	parsley

Fruit

o abacate *oo uh·buh·<u>kaht</u>*	avocado
o abacaxi *oo uh·buh·<u>kah</u>·shee*	pineapple
damascos *oo duh·<u>mahs</u>·koo*	apricots
as ameixas *uhz uh·<u>may</u>·shuhz*	plums
o oxicoco *oo okzee·kaw·koouh*	cranberry
a banana *uh buh·<u>nuh</u>·nuh*	banana
as cerejas *uhz seh·<u>ray</u>·zsuhz*	cherries
o coco *oo <u>kaw</u>·koo*	coconut
a framboesa *uh fruhm·<u>booeh</u>·zuh*	raspberry

a fruta uh <u>froo</u>•tuh	fruit
a goiaba uh goy•<u>ah</u>•buh	guava
o kiwi oo kee•<u>wee</u>	kiwi
a laranja uh luh•<u>ruhn</u>•zsuh	orange
a lima uh <u>lee</u>•muh	lime
o limão oo lee•<u>mohm</u>	lemon
a maçã uh muh•<u>suh</u>	apple
o mamão oo muh•<u>mohm</u>	papaya
a manga uh <u>muhn</u>•guh	mango
a mexerica uh meh•sheh•<u>ree</u>•kuh	tangerine
a melancia uh muh•luhn•<u>see</u>•uh	watermelon
o melão oo meh•<u>lohm</u>	melon
o mirtilo oo meer•<u>tee</u>•loo	blueberry
os morangos ooz moo•<u>ruhn</u>•gooz	strawberries
a pêra uh <u>peh</u>•ruh	pear
o pêssego oo <u>pay</u>•seh•goo	peach
a toranja uh taw•<u>ruhn</u>•zsa	grapefruit
as uvas uhz <u>oo</u>•vuhz	grapes

Cheese

o azeitão oo uh•zay•<u>tohm</u>	creamy cheese
a bola uh <u>bau</u>•luh	hard cow's milk cheese
o cabreiro oo kuh•<u>bray</u>•roo	goat's milk cheese
o castelo branco oo kuh•<u>steh</u>•loo <u>bruhn</u>•koo	creamy blue cheese
a évora uh <u>eh</u>•voo•ruh	creamy cheese
a ilha uh <u>ee</u>•lyuh	cow's milk cheese from the Azores Islands (Portugal)
o queijo oo <u>kay</u>•zsoo	cheese
o queijo de Minas oo•<u>kay</u>•zsoo deh <u>mee</u>•nuhz	Brazilian cow's milk cheese
o requeijão oo reh•kay•<u>zsohm</u>	creamy Brazilian cheese
o serra oo <u>she</u>•rruh	creamy goat's milk cheese

macio muh·_see_·oo	soft
duro _doo_·roo	hard
suave swahv	mild
forte fawrt	strong

Dessert

a arrufada de Coimbra uh uh·rroo·_fah_·duh deh _kooeem_·bruh	cinnamon dough cake
a babá-de-moça uh buh·_bah_ deh _mau_·suh	dessert made of egg yolk, coconut milk and syrup
o bolo podre oo _bau_·loo _pau_·dreh	honey and cinnamon cake
as broas castelares uhz _brau_·uhz kuh·steh·_lah_·rehz	sweet-potato biscuits
a canjica uh _kuhn_·zsee·kuh	dessert made with sweet corn and milk
a goiabada uh goy·uh·_bah_·duh	thick paste made of guavas
a mousse de maracujá uh _moo_·seh deh muh·ruh·koo·_zsah_	passion fruit mousse
os ovos moles ooz _aw_·vooz mawlz	egg yolks cooked in syrup
o pastel de Tentúgal oo puhz·_tehl_ deh tehn·_too_·gahl	pastry filled with egg yolks cooked in syrup
pudim poo·_deeng_	caramel custard
quindim keeng·_deeng_	coconut and egg yolk pudding

Sauces & Condiments

o sal o sahl	salt
a pimenta uh pee·_mehn_·tuh	pepper
mostarda mooz·_tahr_·duh	mustard
ketchup ket·_chup_	ketchup

At the Market

Where are the trolleys/ baskets?	**Onde estão os carrinhos/cestos?**	*aund ee·stohm ooz kuh·rree·nyooz/sehs·tooz*
Where is. . .?	**Onde é. . .?**	*aund eh. . .*
I'd like some of that/ those.	**Queria isso/esses.**	*keh·ree·uh ee·soo/eh·sehz*
Can I taste it?	**Posso provar?**	*paw·soo proo·vahr*
I'd like. . .	**Queria. . .**	*keh·ree·uh. . .*
a kilo/half-kilo of. . .	**um quilo/meio quilo de. . .**	*oong kee·loo/may·oo kee·loo deh. . .*
a liter/half-liter of. . .	**um litro/meio litro de. . .**	*oong lee·troo/may·oo lee·troo deh. . .*
I'd like. . .	**Queria. . .**	*keh·ree·uh. . .*
a piece of. . .	**uma fatia de. . .**	*oo·muh fuh·tee·uh deh. . .*
a slice of. . .	**um pedaço de. . .**	*oong peh·dah·soo deh. . .*
More./Less.	**Mais./Menos.**	*meyez/meh·nooz*
How much?	**Quanto é?**	*kwuhn·too eh*
Where do I pay?	**Onde pago?**	*aund pah·goo*
A bag, please.	**Um saco, por favor.**	*oong sah·koo poor fuh·vaur*
I'm being helped.	**Alguém está·me ajudando.**	*ahl·geng ee·stah meh uh·zsoo·dahn·doo*

YOU MAY HEAR. . .

Deseja alguma coisa? *deh·zeh·zsuh ahl·goo·muh coy·zuh*	Would you like something?
O que é que deseja? *oo kee eh keh deh·zeh·zsuh*	What would you like?
Mais alguma coisa? *meyez ahl·goo·muh coy·zuh*	Anything else?
São. . .reais. *sohm. . .ree·eyez*	That's. . .reais.

In the Kitchen

bottle opener	**o abridor de garrafas** _oo uh•bree•daur deh guh•rrah•fuhz_
bowl	**a tijela** _tee•jeh•lah_
can opener	**o abridor de latas** _oo ah•bree•daur deh lah•tuhz_
corkscrew	**o saca-rolhas** _oo sah•kuh rau•lyuhz_
cups	**as xícaras** _uhz shee•kuh•ruhz_
forks	**os garfos** _ooz gahr•fooz_

Brazil and coffee go hand-in-hand and coffee is one of the country's most successsful exports. Brazilian coffee is roasted dark, ground fine, prepared strong, and drunk with plenty of sugar. **Café com leite** (coffee with hot milk) is the traditional breakfast drink. After breakfast, it is served black in tiny **demitasses** (cups). These **cafezinhos** or little coffees are served piping hot at all **botequins**. Decaffeinated coffee can be found in supermarkets but is difficult to come across in restaurants.

YOU MAY SEE...

USAR ATÉ...	best if used by...
CALORIAS	calories
SEM GORDURA	fat free
MANTER REFRIGERADO	keep refrigerated
PODE CONTER VESTÍGIOS DE...	may contain traces of...
MICROONDAS	microwaveable
DATA DE VENDA...	sell by...
PRÓPRIO PARA VEGETARIANOS	suitable for vegetarians

frying pan	**a frigideira**
	uh free•zsee•<u>thay</u>•ruh
glasses	**os copos**
	ooz <u>kaw</u>•pooz
knife	**as facas**
	uhz <u>fah</u>•kuhz
measuring cup/spoon	**o copo/a colher de medir**
	oo <u>kaw</u>•poo/uh koo•<u>lyehr</u> deh meh•<u>deer</u>
paper napkin	**o guardanapo de papel**
	oo gwahr•duh•<u>nah</u>•poo deh puh•<u>pehl</u>
plates	**os pratos**
	ooz <u>prah</u>•tooz
pot	**a panela**
	uh puh•<u>neh</u>•luh
saucepan	**a caçarola**
	uh kuh•suh•<u>rawl</u>•uh
spatula	**a espátula**
	uh ees•<u>pah</u>•too•luh
spoon	**as colheres**
	uhz koo•<u>lyeh</u>•rehz

ESSENTIAL

The wine list/drink menu, please.	**A carta de vinhos/cardápio de bebidas, por favor.** *uh* <u>*kahr*</u>*·tuh deh* <u>*vee*</u>*·nyooz/car·*<u>*dah*</u>*·pee·oo deh beh·*<u>*bee*</u>*·duhz poor fuh·*<u>*vaur*</u>
What do you recommend?	**O que me recomenda?** *oo keh meh reh·koo·*<u>*mehn*</u>*·duh*
I'd like a bottle/glass of red/white wine.	**Queria uma garrafa/um copo de vinho tinto/branco.** *keh·*<u>*ree*</u>*·uh oo·muh guh·*<u>*rrah*</u>*·fuh/oong* <u>*kaw*</u>*·poo deh* <u>*vee*</u>*·nyoo teen·too/*<u>*bruhn*</u>*·koo*
The house wine, please.	**O vinho da casa, por favor.** *oo* <u>*vee*</u>*·nyoo duh* <u>*kah*</u>*·zuh poor fuh·*<u>*vaur*</u>
Another bottle/glass, please.	**Outra garrafa/Outro copo, por favor.** <u>*auoo*</u>*·truh guh·*<u>*rrah*</u>*·fuh/*<u>*auoo*</u>*·troo* <u>*kaw*</u>*·poo poor fuh·*<u>*vaur*</u>
I'd like a local beer.	**Gostaria de uma cerveja local.** *goo·stuh·*<u>*ree*</u>*·uh deh* <u>*oo*</u>*·muh sehr·*<u>*vay*</u>*·zsuh loo·*<u>*kahl*</u>
Can I buy you a drink?	**Posso oferecer uma bebida?** <u>*paw*</u>*·soo aw·freh·*<u>*sehr*</u> <u>*oo*</u>*·muh beh·*<u>*bee*</u>*·thuh*
Cheers!	**Saúde!** *Sah·ood*
A coffee/tea, please.	**Um café/chá, por favor.** *oong kuh·*<u>*feh*</u>*/shah poor fuh·*<u>*vaur*</u>
Black.	**Cafezinho.** *kuh·feh·*<u>*zee*</u>*·nyoo*
With...	**com...** *kaum...*
milk	**leite** *layt*
sugar	**açúcar** *uh·*<u>*soo*</u>*·kuhr*
artificial sweetener	**adoçante** *uh·doo·*<u>*suhnty*</u>
A..., please.	**..., por favor.** *...por fuh·*<u>*vaur*</u>
juice	**Um suco** *oong* <u>*soo*</u>*·koo*
soda	**Um refrigerante** *oong reh·*<u>*freh*</u>*·zhay·rahnt*

sparkling/still water	**Uma água com/sem gás** _oo_-muh _ah_-gwuh _kaum/sehm gahz_
Is the tap water safe to drink?	**A água da torneira é boa para beber?** _uh ah_-gwuh _duh toor_-_nay_-ruh eh _baw_-uh _puh_-ruh beh-_behr_

Non-alcoholic Drinks

a água de coco _uh ah_-gwuh deh _kau_-koo	coconut juice
a água com/sem gás _uh ah_-gwuh kaum/ sehn gahz	carbonated/ noncarbonated [still] water
o chá frio _oo shah free_-oo	iced tea
o café _oo kuh_-_feh_	coffee
o caldo de cana _oo kahl_-doo deh _kuh_-nuh	sugar-cane juice
o leite _oo layt_	milk
o leite de coco _oo layt deh kau_-koo	coconut milk
o suco _oo soo_-koo	juice
o refrigerante _oo reh_-_free_-zhay-rahnt	soda

YOU MAY HEAR…

Posso oferecer-lhe uma bebida? _paw_-soo aw-freh-_sehr_-lyeh _oo_-muh beh-_bee_-thuh — Can I get you a drink?

Com leite/açúcar? _kaum layt/uh_-_soo_-kuhr — With milk/sugar?

Água com ou sem gás? _ah_-gwuh _kaum auoo seng gahz_ — Carbonated or non-carbonated [still] water?

Look for the bars advertising **suco** (juice) with lots of fresh fruit on display. **Sumol®** is the oldest brand name of fruit juice and is found in almost every shop selling food. It is a lightly carbonated orange drink.

Aperitifs, Cocktails & Liqueurs

aguardente de... *ah·gwahr·thent deh...*	tequila with...
figo *fee·goo*	fig
medronho *meh·draw·nyoo*	arbutus berry (a small strawberry-like fruit)
velha *veh·lyuh*	brandy
a batida... *uh buh·tee·duh...*	cane spirit with fruit juice, sugar, ice and...
de cajú *deh kuh·zsoo*	cashew nut
de coco *deh kau·koo*	coconut
de maracujá *deh muh·ruh·koo·zsah*	passion fruit
a caipirinha *uh keye·pee·ree·nyuh*	cane spirit, crushed lime, sugar and ice
a Cuba livre *uh koo·buh lee·vreh*	rum and Coke®
a gin *uh gzseeng*	gin
a ginjinha *uh zseeng·zsee·nyuh*	spirit distilled from morello cherries
o uísque *oo wees·keh*	whiskey
o vermute *oo vehr·moot*	vermouth
a tequila *uh teh·kee·luh*	tequila
o rum *oo roong*	rum
a vodca *uh vaw·dee·kuh*	vodka

Beer

a cerveja *uh sehr·<u>vay</u>·zsuh*	beer
a cerveja branca *uh sehr·<u>vay</u>·zsuh <u>bruhn</u>·kuh*	lager
a cerveja preta *uh sehr·<u>vay</u>·zsuh <u>preh</u>·tuh*	dark beer
cerveja leve *sehr·<u>veh</u>·zsuh leh·veh*	light beer
um chope *oo <u>shaw</u>·pee*	draft [draught] beer
engarrafada *ehn·<u>guh</u>·rruh·fah·<u>duh</u>*	bottled
local/importada *loo·<u>kahl</u>/eem·<u>pawr</u>·tah·<u>duh</u>*	local imported
sem álcool *seng ahl·<u>kawl</u>*	non-alcoholic

Beer is a popular drink in Brazil. Try local brew **Antártica**. It is often served with **tremoços** (salted lupini beans) or **amendoins** (peanuts). **Cachaça** is the national spirit and comes in varying degrees of quality. It is made from the juice of cane sugar. The very best compare favorably to a top whiskey or brandy. The famous **caipirinha** cocktail is based on this.

Wine

o vinho... *oo <u>vee</u>·nyoo...*	...wine
de casa/mesa *deh <u>kah</u>·zuh/<u>meh</u>·zuh*	house/table
(da) Madeira *(thuh) muh·<u>thay</u>·ruh*	(from) Madeira
(do) Porto *(thoo) <u>paur</u>·too*	Port
espumante *ee·spoo·<u>muhnt</u>*	sparkling
seco/doce *<u>seh</u>·koo/<u>dau</u>·seh*	dry/sweet
tinto/branco/rosé *<u>teen</u>·too/<u>bruhn</u>·koo/ raw·<u>zeh</u>*	red/white/blush [rosé]
verde *vehrd*	dry white wine

Brazil turns out some good red and white wines from its vineyards in the South. Labels to look for include **Almadén** and **Forestier**.

o abacate *oo uh·buh·kaht*	avocado
o abacaxi *oo uh·buh·kah·shee*	pineapple
a abóbora *uh uh·baw·boo·ruh*	pumpkin
o açafrão *oo uh·suh·frohm*	saffron
o acarajé *oo uh·kuh·ruh·zseh*	fried beans
o açúcar *oo uh·soo·kuhr*	sugar
o agrião *oo uh·gree·ohm*	watercress
a água *uh ah·gwuh*	water
a água com gás *uh ah·gwuh kohn gahz*	carbonated mineral water
a água de coco *uh ah·gwuh deh kau·koo*	coconut juice
a água mineral *uh ah·gwuh mee·neh·ral*	mineral water
o aipo *oo ah·ee·poo*	celery
a alcachofra *uh ahl·kuh·shau·fruh*	artichoke
as alcaparras *uhz ahl·kuh·pah·rruhz*	capers
o alecrim *oo uh·leh·kreeng*	rosemary
a aletria *uh uhl·eh·tree·uh*	sweet noodle pudding
a alface *uh ahl·fah·seh*	lettuce
a alheira *uh ah·lwyay·ruh*	sausage
o alho *oo ah·lyoo*	garlic
o alho poró *oo ah·lyoo pau·rroh*	leek
o almoço *oo ahl·mau·soo*	lunch
as almôndegas *uhz ahl·mawn·deh·guhz*	fishballs or meatballs
as amêijoas *uhz uh·may·zsoo·uhz*	baby clams
as ameixas *uhz uh·may·shuhz*	plums
as ameixas secas *uhz uh·may·shuhz seh·kuhz*	prunes
a amêndoa *uh uh·mehn·doo·uh*	almond
o amendoim *oo uh·mehn·doo·eeng*	peanut
a amora *uh uh·maw·ruh*	blackberry
a anchova *uh uhn·shau·vuh*	anchovy

o aperitivo *oo uh‧pehr‧uh‧tee‧voo*	aperitif
o arenque *oo uh‧rehn‧keh*	herring
o arroz *oo uh‧rrauz*	rice
o arroz doce *oo uh‧rrauz dau‧seh*	rice pudding
os aspargos *ooz ees‧pahr‧gooz*	asparagus
o assado *oo uh‧sah‧thoo*	roast
o atum *oo uh‧toong*	tuna
a aveia *uh uh‧vay‧uh*	oats
a avelã *uh uh‧veh‧luh*	hazelnut
as aves *uhz ahv‧ehz*	poultry
a azeda *uh uh‧zeh‧duh*	sorrel
azedo *uh‧zeh‧thoo*	sour
o azeite *oo uh‧zay‧teh*	oil
az azeitonas *uhz uh‧zay‧tau‧nuhz*	olive
o bacalhau *oo buh‧kuh‧lyahoo*	cod
a banana *uh buh‧nuh‧nuh*	banana
a batata *uh buh‧tah‧tuh*	potato
a batata doce *uh buh‧tah‧tuh dau‧seh*	sweet potato
as batatas fritas *uhz buh‧tah‧tuhz free‧tuhz*	fries [chips]
a baunilha *uh bahoo‧nee‧lyuh*	vanilla
a bebida *uh beh‧bee‧thuh*	drink

Portuguese	English
o berbigão oo behr·bee·<u>gohm</u>	type of cockle
a beringela uh behr·eeng·<u>zseh</u>·luh	eggplant [aubergine]
o besugo oo beh·<u>soo</u>·goo	bream(fish)
a beterraba uh beh·teh·<u>rrah</u>·buh	beet [beetroot]
o bife oo beef	steak
o bife acebolado oo beef uh·seh·boo·<u>lah</u>·thoo	steak with onions
a bola de Berlim uh <u>bau</u>·luh deh behr·<u>leeng</u>	doughnut
a bolacha uh boo·<u>lah</u>·shuh	cookie [biscuit]
a bolacha de água e sal uh boo·<u>lah</u>·shuh deh <u>ah</u>·gwuh ee sahl	cracker
o bolo oo <u>bau</u>·loo	pastry
o borrego oo boo·<u>rreh</u>·goo	lamb
as broas de batata doce uhz <u>brau</u>·uhz duh buh·tah·tuh dau·seh	sweet-potato cookies
as broas de mel uhz <u>brau</u>·uhz deh mehl	corn flour and honey cookies
os brócolis ooz <u>braw</u>·koo·looz	broccoli
os bunuelos ooz boo·noo·<u>eh</u>·leez	dough fritters
o cabrito oo kuh·<u>bree</u>·too	kid
a caça uh <u>kah</u>·suh	game
o cacau oo kuh·<u>kahoo</u>	cocoa
o cachorro quente oo kuh·<u>shau</u>·roo kehnt	hot dog
o café oo kuh·<u>feh</u>	coffee
o caju oo kah·<u>zsoo</u>	cashew nut
a caldeirada uh kahl·day·<u>rah</u>·duh	fish stew
o caldo oo <u>kahl</u>·doo	consommé
o caldo de cana oo <u>kahl</u>·doo deh <u>kuh</u>·nuh	sugar-cane juice
o caldo verde oo <u>kahl</u>·doo vehrd	potato and kale soup
os camarões ooz kuh·muh·<u>roings</u>	shrimp
o canapé oo kuh·nuh·<u>peh</u>	small open sandwich
a canela uh kuh·<u>neh</u>·luh	cinnamon
a canja uh <u>keng</u>·juh	chicken soup with rice

o capão *oo cuh·pohm*	capon
o caqui *oo kuh·kee*	persimmon
o caracol *oo kuh·ruh·kawl*	snail; spiral bun with currants
o caranguejo *oo kuh·ruhn·gay·zsoo*	crab
o carapau *oo kuh·ruh·pahoo*	mackerel
o caril *oo kuh·reel*	curry powder
a carne de porco *uh kahr·neh deh paur·koo*	pork
a carne de sol *uh kahr·neh deh sawl*	sun-dried meat, jerky
a carne de vaca *uh kahr·neh deh vah·kuh*	beef
a carne picada *uh kahr·neh pee·kah·thuh*	minced meat
o carneiro *oo kuhrr·nay·roo*	mutton
as carnes *uhz kahr·nehz*	meat
as carnes frias *uhz kahr·nehz free·uhz*	[charcuterie] cold cuts
o caruru *oo kuh·roo·roo*	minced herbs in oil and spices
caseiro *oo kuh·zay·roo*	homemade
a casquinha de siri *uh kuhz·kee·nyuh deh see·ree*	crab in its shell
a castanha *uh kuhz·tuh·nyuh*	chestnut
a castanha de caju *uh kuhz·tuh·nyuh deh kah·zsoo*	cashew nut

a cavala *uh kuh•vuh•luh*	mackerel
a cebola *uh seh•bau•luh*	onion
a cenoura *uh seh•nau•ruh*	carrot
a cereja *uh seh•ray•zsuh*	cherry
o chá *oo shah*	tea
o chá com leite *oo shah kaum layt*	tea with milk
o chá com limão *oo shah kaum lee•mohm*	tea with lemon
o chá de limão *oo shah deh lee•mohm*	tea made from lemon peel infusion
o chá maté *oo shah muh•teh*	tea infused with maté-tree leaf
o cherne *oo shehr•neh*	black grouper
a chicória *uh shee•kaw•ree•uh*	chicory
o chispe *oo sheez•peh*	pig's foot [trotter]
o chocolate quente *oo shoo•koo•laht kehnt*	hot chocolate
os chocos *ooz shau•kooz*	cuttlefish
o chouriço *oo shaw•ree•soo*	smoked pork sausage
o chuchu *oo shoo•shoo*	type of rutabaga
o churrasco *oo shoo•rahz•koo*	charcoal-grilled meat
as cocadas *uhz caw•cah•duhz*	coconut macaroons
o coco *oo kau•koo*	coconut
a codorna *uh koo•dawrr•nuh*	quail
o coelho *oo koo•eh•lyoo*	rabbit
o coentro *oo koo•ehn•troo*	coriander
o cogumelo *oo koo•goo•meh•loo*	button mushroom
o colorau *oo koo•loo•rahoo*	paprika
os cominho *ooz koo•mee•nyoo*	cumin
a compota *uh koom•paw•tuh*	compote, stewed fruit
os condimentos *ooz kaum•dee•mehn•tooz*	seasonings
o congro *oo kaum•groo*	conger eel
o conhaque *oo kaw•nyahk*	cognac

a conta *uh <u>kaum</u>·tuh*	bill
o copo *oo <u>kaw</u>·poo*	glass
o coração *oo koo·ruh·<u>sohm</u>*	heart
o cordeiro *oo koor·<u>day</u>·roo*	lamb
a corvina *uh kawr·<u>vee</u>·nuh*	croaker (fish)
a costeleta *uh koo·stuh·<u>leh</u>·tuh*	cutlet
a couve *uh <u>kaw</u>·veh*	cabbage
a couve Portuguesa *uh <u>kaw</u>·veh poor·too·<u>geh</u>·zuh*	kale
a couve roxa *uh <u>kaw</u>·veh <u>rau</u>·shuh*	red cabbage
a couve-de-bruxelas *uh <u>kaw</u>·veh de broo·<u>sheh</u>·luhz*	brussels sprouts
a couve-flor *uh <u>kaw</u>·veh flaur*	cauliflower
a coxinha de galinha *uh kaw·<u>shee</u>·nyuh deh guh·<u>lee</u>·nyuh*	pastry filled with chicken
os cravinhos *ooz kruh·<u>vee</u>·nyooz*	cloves
o creme *oo krehm*	cream
o creme de abacate *oo krehm deh uh·buh·<u>kaht</u>*	avocado with lime juice and sugar
o creme inglês *oo krehm eeng·laez*	custard
o crepe *oo krehp*	pancake
a criação *uh kree·uh·<u>sohm</u>*	poultry
cru *kroo*	raw
os crustáceos *ooz kroo·<u>stah</u>·see·ooz*	shellfish
o damasco *oo duh·<u>mahs</u>·koo*	apricot
a dendê *uh dehn·<u>deh</u>*	palm oil
o doce de abóbora *oo thaus deh uh·<u>baw</u>·boo·ruh*	pumpkin dessert
a geleia *uh zseh·<u>lay</u>·uh*	jam
o doce de laranja *oo thaus de luh·<u>ruhn</u>·zsuh*	marmalade

o doce de ovos e amêndoa *oo thaus deh aw·vooz ee uh·mehn·doo·uh* — marzipan

a empadinha *uh eem·puh·thee·nyuh* — filled pastry

o empadão de batata *oo eem·puh·dohm deh buh·tah·tuh* — shepherd's pie

empanado *ehm·puh·nah·doo* — breaded

a enguia *uh eng·gee·uh* — eel

o ensopado de cabrito *oo eng·soo·pah·thoo deh keh·bree·too* — kid stew

a entrada *uh ehn·trah·thuh* — appetizer [starter]

o entrecosto *oo ehn·treh·kaus·too* — sparerib

a erva-doce *uh ehr·vuh thaus* — aniseed

as ervilhas *uhz eer·vee·lyuhz* — peas

escalfado *ee·skahl·fah·thoo* — poached

o espadarte *oo ee·spah·dahr·teh* — swordfish

o espaguete *oo ee·spah·geht* — spaghetti

os espinafres *ooz ee·spee·nah·frehz* — spinach

estufado *ee·stoo·fah·thoo* — braised

o esturjão *oo ee·stoor·zsohm* — sturgeon

o faisão *oo feye·zohm* — pheasant

a farinha *uh fuh·ree·nyuh* — flour

a farofa *uh fuh·rau·fuh* — cassava flour

as favas *uhz fah·vuhz* — broad beans

o feijão *oo fay·zsohm* — bean

o feijão branco *oo fay·zsohm bruhn·koo* — navy bean

o feijão catarino *oo fay·zsohm kuh·tuh·ree·noo* — pink bean

o feijão encarnado *oo fay·zsohm eng·kuhrr·nah·thoo* — red bean

o feijão frade *oo fay·zsohm frahd* — black-eyed bean

o feijão guisado [ensopado] *oo fay·zsohm gee·sah·thoo [een·soo·pah·doo]* — beans with bacon in tomato sauce

o feijão preto *oo fay-zsohm preh-too*		black bean
o feijão tropeiro *oo fay-zsohm trau-pay-roo*		black beans fried with jerky
o feijão verde *oo fay-zsohm vehrd*		green beans
o fiambre *oo fee-uhm-breh*		boiled ham
o fígado *oo fee-guh-doo*		liver
o figo *oo fee-goo*		fig
o filé *oo fee-leh*		steak
o filete *oo fee-leht*		fillet of fish
o folhado *oo foo-lyah-thoo*		sweet puff-pastry
as filhós *uhz fee-lyawz*		fritters
a framboesa *uh fruhm-boo-eh-zuh*		raspberry
o frango *oo fruhn-goo*		chicken
o frango assado *oo fruhn-goo uh-sah-thoo*		roast chicken
a fritada de peixe *uh free-tah-duh deh paysh*		deep-fried fish
a fruta *uh froo-tuh*		fruit
a fruta do conde *uh froo-tuh thoo kaum-deh*		custard apple
a fruta em calda *uh froo-tuh eng kahl-duh*		fruit in syrup
os frutos do mar *ooz froo-tuhz thoo mahr*		seafood
a fubá *uh foo-bah*		corn flour
a galantina *uh guh-luhn-tee-nuh*		pressed meat in gelatin
o galão *oo guh-lohm*		weak milky coffee
a galinha *uh guh-lee-nyuh*		stewing chicken
a galinhola *uh guh-lee-nyaw-luh*		woodcock
o ganso *oo guhn-soo*		goose
a garoupa *uh guh-rauoo-puh*		large grouper (fish)
a garrafa *uh guh-rrah-fuh*		bottle
a gasosa *uh guh-zaw-zuh*		lemonade
o gaspacho *oo guhz-pah-shoo*		chilled soup
a gelatina *uh zseh-luh-tee-nuh*		jelly
a geleia *uh zseh-lay-uh*		jelly
o gelo *oo zseh-loo*		ice

o gengibre *oo zsehn-zsee-breh*	ginger
a goiaba *uh zsoy-ah-buh*	guava
a goiabada *uh zsoy-uh-bah-duh*	thick paste made of guava
o gombo *oo gaum-boo*	okra
os grelos *ooz greh-looz*	turnip sprouts
a groselha *uh groo-zeh-lyuh*	red currant
o guisado *oo gee-zah-thoo*	stew
a hortaliça *uh awr-tuh-lee-suh*	fresh vegetables
a hortelã *uh awr-teh-luh*	mint
o inhame *oo ee-nuhm*	yam
o iogurte *oo yaw-goort*	yogurt
a isca de peixe *uh ees-kuh deh paysh*	fried small fish
as iscas *uhz ees-kuhz*	sliced liver
a jabuticaba *uh juh-boo-tee-cah-buh*	type of cherry
a jardineira *uh zsuhr-dee-nay-ruh*	mixed vegetables
o javali *oo zsuh-vah-li*	wild boar
o kibe *oo keeb*	meat and bulgur croquette
o kiwi *oo kee-vee*	kiwi
a lagosta *uh lah-gau-stuh*	lobster
o lagostim *oo luh-gau-steeng*	crayfish
lagostim do-rio *luh-gau-steeng doo ree-oo*	fresh-water crayfish
a lampreia *uh luhm-pray-uh*	lamprey
a laranja *uh luh-ruhn-zsuh*	orange
a laranjada *uh luh-ruhn-zsah-thuh*	orange soda
a lebre *uh leh-breh*	hare
os legumes *ooz leh-goomz*	vegetables
o leite *oo layt*	milk
o leite de coco *oo layt deh kau-koo*	coconut milk
o leitão *oo lay-tohm*	suckling pig
as lentilhas *uhz lehn-tee-lyuhz*	lentils
a lima *uh lee-muh*	lime

o limão *oo lee·mohm*	lemon
o limão verde *oo lee·mohm vehrd*	lime
a língua *uh leen·gwuh*	tongue
o linguado *oo leen·gwah·doo*	sole
a linguiça *uh leen·gwee·suh*	thin sausage
o lombo *oo laum·boo*	loin
o louro *oo lau·roo*	bay leaf
a lula *uh loo·luh*	squid
a maçã *uh muh·suh*	apple
o macarrão *oo muh·kuh·rrohm*	macaroni
a macaxeira *uh muh·kuh·shay·ruh*	cassava root
maduro *muh·thoo·roo*	ripe
a maionese *uh meye·aw·nehz*	mayonnaise
a malagueta *uh muh·luh·geh·tuh*	hot pepper
as malsadas *uhz mahl·sah·duhz*	fried dough
o mamão *oo muh·mohm*	papaya
a mandioca *uh muhn·dee·aw·kuh*	cassava root
a manga *uh muhn·guh*	mango
o manjericão *oo muhn·zsehr·ee·kohm*	basil
a manteiga *uh muhn·tay·guh*	butter
o maracujá *oo muh·ruh·koo·zsah*	passion fruit
os mariscos *ooz muh·rees·kooz*	seafood
a marmelada *uh muhr·meh·lah·duh*	thick quince paste
a massa *uh mah·suh*	pasta; dough; pastry
o marzipã *oo marh·zee·pahn*	marzipan
o mate *oo maht*	tea with maté leaf
o medalhão *oo meh·deh·lyohm*	tenderloin steak
o medronho *oo meh·drau·nyoo*	arbutus berry (small strawberry-like fruit)
o mel *oo mehl*	honey
a melancia *uh muh·luhn·see·uh*	watermelon

o melão *oo meh•lohm*	melon
o melão com presunto *oo meh•lohm kaumpreh•zoon•too*	melon with ham
o mero *oo meh•roo*	red grouper (fish)
a mexerica *uh meh•sheh•ree•kuh*	tangerine
os mexilhões *ooz meh•shee•lyoings*	mussels
a sopa de bacalhau *uh saw•puh deh buh•kuh•lyahoo*	dried cod soup
o milho *oo mee•lyoo*	sweet corn
o milkshake *oo milk•shake*	milk shake
os miolos *ooz mee•aw•looz*	brains
o misto quente *oo mee•stoo kehnt*	ham-and-cheese toasted sandwich
o morango *oo moo•ruhn•goo*	strawberry
a morcela *uh moor•seh•luh*	blood sausage [black pudding]
a mortadela *uh moor•tuh•deh•luh*	mortadella
a mostarda *uh moo•stahr•duh*	mustard
a mousse de chocolate *uh moo•seh deh shoo•koo•laht*	chocolate pudding
a mousse de maracujá *uh moo•seh deh muh•ruh•koo•zsah*	passion fruit mousse
as nabiças *uhz nuh•bee•suhz*	turnip greens
os nabos *ooz nah•booz*	turnips
o creme *oo krehm*	fresh cream
a creme batido *uh krehm buh•tee•duh*	whipped cream
(ao) natural *(ahoo) nuh•too•rahl*	plain
as nêsperas *uhz neh•speh•ruhz*	loquat (fruit)
no forno *noo faurr•noo*	baked
a noz *uh nawz*	nut
a noz moscada *uh nawz moo•skah•thuh*	nutmeg

o óleo *oo aw·lee·oo*	oil
o óleo de amendoim *oo aw·lee·oo deh uh·mehn·doo·eeng*	peanut oil
a omelete *uh aw·meh·leht*	omelet
o orégano *oo aw·re·ga·noom*	oregano
o osso *oo au·soo*	bone
a ostra *uh aw·struh*	oyster
o ovo *oo aw·voo*	egg
os ovos cozidos *ooz aw·vooz koo·zee·thooz*	boiled eggs
os ovos escalfados *ooz aw·vooz ees·kahl·fah·thooz*	poached eggs
os ovos estrelados [fritos] *ooz aw·vooz ees·truh·lah·dooz [free·tooz]*	fried eggs
os ovos mexidos *ooz aw·vooz meh·shee·dooz*	scrambled eggs
os ovos quentes *ooz aw·vooz kehntz*	soft-boiled eggs
o palmito *oo pahl·mee·too*	palmhearts
a panqueca *uh puhn·keh·kuh*	pancake
o pão (escuro/integral) *oo pohm (ees·koo·roo/een·teh·grahl)*	bread (brown/whole wheat)
o pão de centeio *oo pohm deh sehn·tay·oo*	rye bread
o pão-de-ló *oo pohm·deh·law*	coffee cake
o pãozinho *oo pohm·zee·nyoo*	bread roll
o pargo *oo pahr·goo*	bream (fish)
as passas (de uva) *uhz pah·suhz (deh oo·vuh)*	raisin
passado *puh·sah·thoo*	cooked (meat, etc.)
o pastel *oo puhs·tehl*	small pie
o pato *oo pah·too*	duck
o pé de moleque *oo peh deh maw·leh·keh*	peanut brittle
o peito de galinha *oo pay·too deh guh·lee·nyuh*	chicken breast

o peixe *oo paysh*	fish
o peixe-agulha *oo paysh·uh·goo·lya*	garfish
o peixe-espada *oo paysh ees·pah·duh*	swordfish
o pepino *oo peh·pee·noo*	cucumber
o pepino em conserva *oo peh·pee·noo em kaum·sehr·vuh*	pickle [gherkin]
a pêra *uh peh·ruh*	pear
a perca *uh pehr·kuh*	perch
a perdiz *uh pehr·deez*	partridge
a perna de galinha *uh pehrr·nuh deh guh·lee·nyuh*	chicken leg
o pernil *oo perr·neel*	ham
o pero *oo peh·rau*	variety of apple
o peru *oo peh·roo*	turkey
os pés de porco *ooz pehz deh paur·koo*	pig's feet [trotters]
a pescada *uh pehz·kah·thuh*	whiting
o pêssego *oo peh·suh·goo*	peach
os petiscos *ooz peh·tees·kooz*	appetizers [starters]
a pevide *uh peh·veed*	salted pumpkin seed
a picanha desfiada *uh pee·kuh·nyuh dehs·fee·ah·thuh*	charcoal-grilled meat

os picles *ooz pee·kehlz* — pickled vegetables

a pimenta *uh pee·mehn·tuh* — pepper

os pimentões assados *ooz pee·mehn·tooz uh·sah·dooz* — roasted peppers

o pinhão *oo pee·nyohm* — nut

a pinhoada *uh pee·nyoo·ah·duh* — pine nut brittle

o pipis *oo pee·peez* — spicy giblet stew

o pirarucu *oo pee·ruh·roo·koo* — type of fish

o piri-piri *oo pee·ree pee·ree* — seasoning of hot chili pepper and olive oil

o polvo *oo paul·voo* — octopus

o pombo *oo paum·boo* — pigeon

o porco *oo paur·koo* — pork

a posta *uh paws·tuh* — slice of fish or meat

o presunto *oo preh·zoon·too* — cured ham

o presunto cru *oo preh·zoon·too kroo* — dried ham

o pudim *oo poo·deeng* — caramel custard

o puré de batatas *oo poo·reh deh buh·tah·tuhz* — mashed potatoes

a queijada *uh kay·zsah·duh* — small cottage-cheese tart

o queijinho do céu *oo kay·zsee·nyoo doo sehoo* — marzipan balls rolled in sugar

o queijo *oo kay·zsoo* — cheese

o quiabo *oo kee·ah·boo* — okra

o quindim *oo keeng·deeng* — pudding made with coconut and egg yolks

a rabanada *uh ruh·buh·nah·duh* — French toast

o rabanete *oo ruh·buh·neht* — radish

a raia *uh reye·uh* — skate (fish)

a rainha-cláudia *uh ray·ee·nyuh klaw·dee·uh* — greengage plum

recheado *reh·shee·ah·thoo* — stuffed

o recheio *oo re·shay·oo*	stuffing
o refogado *oo reh·foo·gah·thoo*	onions fried in olive oil
o refrigerante *oo reh·free·zsay·rahnt*	soft drink
o repolho *oo rreh·pau·lyoo*	cabbage
o requeijão *oo rre·kay·zsohm*	curd cheese
o rim *oo rreeng*	kidney
o robalo *oo rraw·buh·loo*	sea bass
o rodízio *oo rroo·dee·zee·oo*	selection of chargrilled meats
a romã *uh rrau·muh*	pomegranate
a rosca *uh rraus·kuh*	ring-shaped white bread
o rosmaninho *oo rrooz·muh·neeng·nyoo*	rosemary
o ruivo *oo rroo·ee·voo*	red gurnard (fish)
o sal *oo sahl*	salt
a salada *uh suh·lah·duh*	salad
a salada de alface/escarola *uh suh·lah·duh deh ahl·fah·seh/ees·kuh·raw·luh*	green salad
a salada de agrião *uh suh·lah·duh deh uh·gree·ohm*	watercress salad
a salada mista *uh suh·lah·duh mees·tuh*	tomato and lettuce salad
salgado *sahl·gah·thoo*	salted
o salmão (defumado) *oo suh·mohm (deh·foo·mah·do)*	(smoked) salmon
o salmonete *oo sahl·moo·neht*	red mullet
a salsa *uh sahl·suh*	parsley
a salsicha *uh sahl·see·shuh*	sausage
salteado *sahl·tee·ah·thoo*	sautéed
a sálvia *uh sahl·vee·uh*	sage
as sandes *uhz suhndz*	sandwich
o sanduíche *oo suhn·doo·eesh*	sandwich
a santola *uh suhn·taw·luh*	spider-crab
o sarapatel *oo suh·ruh·puh·tehl*	pork or mutton stew

a sarda *uh <u>sahr</u>·thuh*	mackerel
as sardinhas *uhz suhr·<u>dee</u>·nyuhz*	sardines
o sável *oo <u>sah</u>·vehl*	shad (herring-like fish)
seco <u>seh</u>·koo	dry
a sêmola *uh <u>seh</u>·moo·luh*	semolina
o suflê de canela *oo soo·<u>flay</u> duh cuh·<u>neh</u>·lah*	cinnamon soufflé
a sidra *uh <u>see</u>·druh*	cider
o siri *oo <u>see</u>·ree*	crab
as sobremesas *uhz <u>sau</u>·breh·<u>meh</u>·zuhz*	dessert
a solha *uh <u>sau</u>·lyuh*	plaice (fish)
o sonho *oo <u>sau</u>·nyoo*	type of doughnut
a sopa *uh <u>sau</u>·puh*	soup
o sorvete *oo sawr·<u>veht</u>*	ice cream
o suco *oo <u>soo</u>·koo*	fruit juice
o sururu *oo soo·<u>roo</u>·roo*	type of cockle
o suspiro *oo soo·<u>spee</u>·roo*	meringue
a taínha *uh tah·<u>ee</u>·nyuh*	gray mullet (fish)
a tâmara *uh <u>tuh</u>·muh·ruh*	date
a tangerina *uh tuhn·zsuh·<u>ree</u>·nuh*	tangerine
a torta de amêndoa *uh tohr·tah de uh·<u>mehn</u>·doo·uh*	almond tart
o tempero *oo <u>tehm</u>·peh·roo*	seasoning
tenro <u>tehn</u>·rroo	tender
o tomate *oo too·<u>maht</u>*	tomato
o tomilho *oo too·<u>mee</u>·lyoo*	thyme
a toranja *uh tau·<u>ruhn</u>·zsuh*	grapefruit
as torradas *uhz too·<u>rrah</u>·duhz*	toast
o torrão de ovos *oo too·<u>rrohm</u> deh <u>aw</u>·vooz*	marzipan candy
a tosta *uh <u>taw</u>·stuh*	toasted sandwich
o toucinho *oo tau·<u>see</u>·nyoo*	bacon
o tremoço *oo treh·<u>maw</u>·soo*	salted lupin bean

a trufa *uh <u>troo</u>·fuh*	truffle
a truta *uh <u>troo</u>·tuh*	trout
o tucupi *oo too·<u>koo</u>·pee*	cassava juice
o tutano *oo <u>too</u>·tuh·noo*	marrow
o umbu *oo <u>oom</u>·boo*	tropical fruit
as uvas *uhz <u>oo</u>·vuhz*	grapes
as vagens *uhz <u>vah</u>·gehnz*	green beans
variado *vuh·ree·<u>ah</u>·thoo*	assorted
o veado *oo vee·<u>ah</u>·thoo*	venison
os vegetais variados *ooz veh·zseh·<u>teyez</u>* *vuh·ree·<u>ah</u>·thooz*	mixed vegetables
a vieira *uh vee·<u>ay</u>·ruh*	scallop
o vinagre *oo vee·<u>nah</u>·greh*	vinegar
a vitela *uh vee·<u>tehl</u>·uh*	veal

People

Conversation

ESSENTIAL

Hello.	**Oi.** _au_-hee
How are you?	**Tudo bem?** Too-duh beng
Fine, thanks.	**Bem, obrigado _m_ /obrigada _f_.** behm aw-bree-_gah_-doo/aw-bree-_gah_-duh
Excuse me!	**Desculpe!** dehz-_kool_-peh
Do you speak English?	**Fala inglês?** _fah_-luh eeng-_lehz_
What's your name?	**Como se chama?** _kau_-moo seh _shuh_-muh
My name is...	**Meu nome é...** mehoo _naum_-ee eh...
Nice to meet you.	**Muito prazer.** _mooee_-too pruh-_zehr_
Where are you from?	**De onde é?** deh aund eh
I'm from the U.S./U.K.	**Sou dos Estados Unidos/da Inglaterra.** soh dooz ee-_stah_-dooz oo-_nee_-dooz/ duh eeng-luh-_teh_-rruh
What do you do?	**O que é que faz?** oo kee eh keh fahz
I work for...	**Trabalho para...** truh-_bah_-lyoo puh-ruh...
I'm a student.	**Sou estudante.** sauoo ee-stoo-_duhnt_
I'm retired.	**Sou aposentado _m_ /aposentada _f_.** soh uh-poo-zehn-_tah_-doo/uh-poo-zehn-_tah_-duh
Do you like...?	**Gosta de...?** _gaw_-stuh deh...
Goodbye.	**Tchau.** chah-oo
See you later.	**Até mais tarde.** uh-_teh_ meyez tahrd

Você is predominantly used for "you" when talking to anyone, regardless of age or class. **Você(s)** takes either the third person singular or the third person plural of the verb depending on whether you're referring to one person (**você**) or more than one person (**vocês**).

Language Difficulties

Do you speak English?	**Fala inglês?** _fah_•luh eeng•_lehz_
Does anyone here speak English?	**Alguém que fale inglês?** _ahl_•_gehng_ keh _fah_•leh eeng•_lehz_
I don't speak (much) Portuguese.	**Não falo (muito) português.** nohm _fah_•loo (mooee•too) poor•too•_gehz_
Could you speak more slowly?	**Pode falar mais devagar?** pawd fuh•_lahr_ meyez deh•vuh•_gahr_
Could you repeat that?	**Pode repetir?** pawd reh•peh•_teer_
Excuse me? [Pardon?]	**Desculpe?** dehz•_kool_•peh
What was that?	**Como disse?** _kau_•moo _dee_•seh
Could you spell it?	**Pode soletrar?** pawd sau•leh•_trahr_
Please write it down.	**Escreva, por favor.** ee•_screhv_ poor fuh•_vaur_
Can you translate this for me?	**Pode traduzir isto?** pawd truh•doo•_zeer_ ee•stoo
What does this/that mean?	**O que significa isto/aquilo?** oo keh sehg•nee•_fee_•kuh ee•stoo/uh•_kee_•loo
I understand.	**Entendo.** ehn•_tehn_•doo
I don't understand.	**Não entendo.** nohm ehn•_tehn_•doo
Do you understand?	**Entende?** ehn•_tehn_•deh

For Communications, see page 52.

YOU MAY HEAR...

Falo só um pouco de Inglês. *fah·loo saw oong pau·koo deh eeng·lehz*
I only speak a little English.

Nao falo Inglês. *nohm fah·loo eeng·lehz*
I don't speak English.

Making Friends

Hello.	**Oi.** *Au·hee*
Good morning.	**Bom dia.** *bong dee·uh*
Good afternoon.	**Boa tarde.** *baw·uh tahrd*
Good evening.	**Boa noite.** *baw·uh noyt*
My name is...	**Meu nome é...** *mehoo naum·ee eh...*
What's your name?	**Como se chama?** *kau·moo seh shuh·muh*
I'd like to introduce you to...	**Gostaria de te apresentar ao/à...** *goo·stuh·ree·uh deh the uh·preh·sehn·tahr ahoo/ah...*
Nice to meet you.	**Muito prazer.** *mooee·too preh·zehr*
How are you?	**Como está?** *kau·moo ee·stah*
Fine, thanks.	**Bem, obrigado m /obrigada f.** *beng aw·bree·gah·doo/aw·bree·gah·duh*
And you?	**E o senhor m /a senhora f?** *ee oo seh·nyaur/uh seh·nyau·ruh*

In Brazil, a standard greeting is a handshake accompanied by direct eye contact and the appropriate greeting for the time of day. Once a closer relationship has developed, greetings become more personal: men may greet each other with a hug, and women kiss each other twice on the cheek starting on the right-hand side. Brazilians often use a first name with a title of respect: **Senhor** for men, **Senhora** or **Dona** for women. Wait until invited before moving to a first-name basis.

Travel Talk

I'm here...	**Estou aqui...** ee·_stawoo_ uh·_kee_...
on business	**a negócios** ah neh·_gaw_·see·yooz
on vacation [holiday]	**de férias** deh _feh_·ree·uhz
studying	**estudando** ee·stoo·_duhn_·doo
I'm staying for...	**Fico por...** _fee_·koo poor...
I've been here...	**Eu já estive aqui...** ehoo zsah ee·_stee_·veh uh·_kee_...
a day	**um dia** oong _dee_·uh
a week	**uma semana** _oo_·muh seh·_muh_·nuh
a month	**um mês** oong mehz
Where are you from?	**De onde é?** deh aund eh
I'm from...	**Sou...** sawoo...

For Numbers, see page 173.

Personal

Who are you with?	**Com quem está?** kaun keng ee·_stah_
I'm on my own.	**Estou sozinho** *m* /**sozinha** *f.* ee·_stawoo_ saw·_zee_·nyoo/saw·_zee_·nyuh
I'm with my...	**Estou com o meu** *m* /**a minha** *f*... ee·_stawoo_ kaum oo mehoo/uh _mee_·nyuh...

husband/wife	**marido/mulher** *muh·ree·thoo/moo·lyehr*	
boyfriend/girlfriend	**namorado/namorada** *nuh·moo·rah·thoo/ nuh·moo·rah·thuh*	
friend(s)	**amigo(s) _m_ /amiga(s) _f_** *uh·mee·goo(z)/ uh·mee·guh(z)*	
colleague(s)	**colega(s)** *koo·leh·guh(z)*	
When's your birthday?	**Quando faz aniversário?** *kwuhn·doo fahz uh·ni·vehr·sah·ree·oo*	
How old are you?	**Quantos anos tem?** *kwuhn·tooz uh·noos teng*	
I'm...	**Eu tenho...** *ehoo teh·nyoo...*	
Are you married?	**É casado _m_ /casada _f_?** *eh kuh·zah·doo/kuh·zah·duh*	
I'm...	**Sou.../Estou...** *sawoo/ee·stawoo...*	
single	**solteiro _m_ /solteira _f_** *saul·tay·roo/(saul·tay·ruh)*	
in a relationship	**num relacionamento** *noong reh·luh·see·oo·nuh·mehn·too*	
I'm...	**Sou.../Estou...** *sawoo/ee·stawoo...*	
engaged	**comprometido** *kaum·proo·meh·tee·doo*	
married	**casado _m_ /casada _f_** *kuh·zah·doo/kuh·zah·duh*	
divorced	**divorciado _m_ /divorciada _f_** *dee·voor·see·ah·doo/ dee·voor·see·ah·duh*	
separated	**separado _m_ /separada _f_** *seh·puh·rah·doo/ seh·puh·rah·duh*	
I'm widowed.	**Sou viúvo _m_ /viúva _f_.** *sau vee·oo·voo/vee·oo·vuh*	
Do you have children/ grandchildren?	**Tem filhos/netos?** *teng fee·lyooz/neh·tooz*	

Work & School

What do you do?	**O que é que faz?** *oo kee eh keh fahz*
What are you studying?	**O que é que está estudando?** *oo kee eh keh ee·stah ee·stoo·duhn·doo*

I'm studying...	**Estudo...** *ee·stoo·doo...*
I work full time/ part time.	**Trabalho tempo período/meio tempo.** *truh·bah·lyoo tehm·poo puh·ree·ooduh/may·oo tehm·poo*
I'm between jobs.	**Estou entre empregos.** *ee·stawoo ehn·treh ehng·preh·gooz*
I'm unemployed.	**Estou desempregado.** *ee·stawoo deh·zehm·preh·gah·doo.*
I work at home.	**Trabalho em casa.** *truh·bah·lyoo eng kah·zuh*
Who do you work for?	**Para quem trabalha?** *puh·ruh keng truh·bah·lyuh*
I work for...	**Trabalho para...** *truh·bah·lyoo puh·ruh...*
Here's my business card.	**Aqui está meu cartão.** *uh·kee ee·stah mehoo kuhr·tohm*

Weather

What's the weather forecast?	**Quais são as previsões do tempo?** *kweyez sohm uhz preh·vee·zoings thoo tehm·poo*
What beautiful/ terrible weather!	**Que tempo tão lindo/ruim!** *keh tehm·poo tohm leen·doo/rroo·eeng*
It's cool/warm.	**Está fresco/calor.** *ee·stah frehs·koo/kuh·laur*
It's hot/cold.	**Está calor/frio.** *ee·stah kuh·laur/free·oo.*
It's rainy/sunny.	**Está um dia de chuva/sol.** *ee·stah oong dee·uh deh shoo·vuh/sawl*
It's snowy/icy.	**Está um dia de neve/com gelo.** *ee·stah oong dee·uh deh nehv/kaum zseh·loo*
Do I need a jacket/ an umbrella?	**Preciso de um casaco/guarda-chuva?** *preh·see·zoo deh oong kuh·zah·koo/goo·ahr·dah shoo·vuh*

ESSENTIAL

Would you like to go out for a drink/dinner?	**Quer tomar uma bebida/comer fora?** _kehr too·mahr oo·muh beh·bee·thuh/koo·mehr faw·ruh_
What are your plans for tonight/tomorrow?	**Quais são os seus planos para hoje à noite/amanhã?** _kweyez sohm ooz sehooz pluh·nooz puh·ruh auzseh ah noyt/uh·muh·nyuh_
Can I have your number?	**Qual o seu número de telefone?** _Kwal oo seoh noo·meh·roo deh tehl·fawn_
Can I join you?	**Posso te acompanhar?** _paw·soo teh uh·kaum·puh·nyahr_
Can I buy you a drink?	**O que quer beber?** _oo keh kehr beh·behr_
I like you.	**Gosto de você.** _gawzh·too deh voh·seh_
I love you.	**Te amo.** _teh uh·moo_

The Dating Game

Would you like to go out for...?	**Quer sair para...?** _kehr seh·eer puh·ruh..._
coffee	**um café** _oong kuh·feh_
a drink	**uma bebida** _oo·muh beh·bee·thuh_
dinner	**jantar** _zsuhn·tahr_
What are your plans for...?	**Quais são os seus planos para...?** _kweyez sohm ooz sehooz pluh·nooz puh·ruh..._
tonight	**hoje à noite** _auzseh ah noyt_
tomorrow	**amanhã** _uh·muh·nyuh_
this weekend	**este fim de semana** _ehst feeng deh seh·muh·nuh_

Where would you like to go?	**Onde quer ir?** *aund kehr eer*
I'd like to go to…	**Quero ir à…** *keh•roo eer ah…*
Do you like…?	**Gosta de…?** *gaw•stuh deh…*
Can I have your number/e-mail?	**Podes me dar o seu número de telefone/e-mail?** *pawd•ehz meh dahr oo sehoo noo•meh•roo deh tehl•fawn /ee•mehl*
Are you on Facebook/Twitter?	**Está no Facebook/Twitter?** *ee•stah noo facebook/twitter*
Can I join you?	**Posso te acompanhar?** *paw•soo teh uh•kaum•puh•nyahr*
You look great!	**Está linda!** *ee•stah leen•duh*
Let's go somewhere quieter.	**Vamos para um lugar mais sossegado.** *vuh•mooz puh•ruh oong loo•gahr meyez soo•seh•gah•thoo*

For Communications, see page 52.

Accepting & Rejecting

I'd love to.	**Adoraria ir.** *uh•doo•ruh•ree•uh eer*
Where should we meet?	**Onde vamos nos encontrar?** *aund vuh•mooz nooz ehng•kaun•trahr*

I'll meet you at the bar/ your hotel.	**Vou te encontrar no bar/hotel.** *vauoo tee ehn·kaun·trahr noo bahr/aw·tehl*
I'll come by at…	**Eu passo por lá às…** *ehoo pah·soo poor lah ahz…*
What's your address?	**Qual é o suo endereço?** *kwahl eh uh soo·uh ehn·deh·reh·soo*
I'm busy.	**Mas tenho muito que fazer.** *muhz teh·nyoo mooee·too keh fuh·zehr*
I'm not interested.	**Não estou interessado *m* /interessada *f*.** *nohm ee·stawoo een·treh·sah·thoo/een·treh·sah·thuh*
Leave me alone.	**Me deixe em paz.** *meh day·sheh eng pahz*
Stop bothering me!	**Páre!** *pah·reeee*

Getting Intimate

Can I hug/kiss you?	**Posso te dar um abraço/beijo?** *paw·soo teh dahr oong uh·brah·soo/bay·zsoo*
Yes.	**Sim.** *seeng*
No.	**Não.** *nohm*
Stop!	**Pára!** *pah·ruh*
I love you.	**Te amo.** *teh uh·moo*

Sexual Preferences

Are you gay?	**Você é homossexual?** *Voh·seh eh aw·maw·sehk·soo·ahl*
I'm…	**Sou…** *sauoo…*
heterosexual	**heterossexual** *eh·teh·raw·sehk·soo·ahl*
homosexual	**homossexual** *aw·maw·sehk·soo·ahl*
bisexual	**bissexual** *bee·sehk·soo·ahl*
Do you like men/ women?	**Gosta de homens/mulheres?** *gaw·stuh deh aw·mengz/moo·lyehrz*

For Grammar, see page 169.

Leisure Time

Sightseeing

ESSENTIAL

Where's the tourist office?	**Onde é o posto de informações turísticas?** *aund eh oo pau•stoo deh een•foor•muh•soings too•ree•stee•kuhz*
What are the main points of interest?	**O que há de mais interessante para se ver?** *oo kee ah deh meyez een•tehr•reh•suhnt puh•ruh seh vehr*
Do you have tours in English?	**Tem excursões em inglês?** *teng ee•skoor•soings eng eng•lehz*
Can I have a map/guide?	**Pode me dar um mapa/guia?** *pawd meh dahr oong mah•puh/ gee•uh*

Tourist Information

Do you have any information on...?	**Tem informação sobre...?** *teng een•foor•muh•sohm sau•breh...*
Can you recommend...?	**Pode recomendar...?** *pawd reh•koo•mehn•dahr...*
a boat trip	**uma excursão de barco** *oo•muh ee•skoor•sohm deh bahr•koo*
an excursion	**uma excursão** *oo•muh ee•skoor•sohm*
a sightseeing tour	**um circuito turístico** *oong seer•koo•ee•too too•ree•stee•koo*

For Disabled Travelers, see page 153.

Town maps and brochures on main tourist attractions are available at airports and from tourist information centers. Ask at your hotel or check online to find the nearest office.

On Tour

I'd like to go on the tour to...	**Gostaria de ir na excursão para...** _goo•stuh•<u>ree</u>•uh deh eer nuh ee•skoor•<u>sohm</u> puh•ruh..._
When's the next tour?	**Quando é a próxima excursão?** _kwuhn•doo eh uh <u>praw</u>•see•muh ee•skoor•<u>sohm</u>_
Are there tours in English?	**Há excursões em inglês?** _ah ee•skoor•<u>soings</u> eng eeng•<u>lehz</u>_
Is there an English-speaking guide/audio guide?	**Há algum guia que fale inglês/uma gravação da visita guiada em inglês?** _ah ahl•<u>goong</u> gee•uh keh <u>fah</u>•leh eeng•<u>lehz</u>/<u>oo</u>•muh gruh•vuh•<u>sohm</u> deh vee•<u>zee</u>•tuh gee•<u>ah</u>•duh eng eeng•<u>lehz</u>_
What time do we leave/return?	**Quando saímos/regressemos?** _kwuhn•doo suh•<u>eemooz</u>/reh•<u>greh</u>•seh•mooz_
We'd like to see...	**Gostaríamos de ver...** _goo•stuh•<u>ree</u>•uh•mooz deh vehr..._
Can we stop here...?	**Podemos parar aqui...?** _poo•<u>deh</u>•mooz puh•<u>rahr</u> uh•<u>kee</u>..._
to take photographs	**para tirar fotografias** _puh•ruh tee•<u>rahr</u> foo•too•gruh•<u>fee</u>•uhz_
to buy souvenirs	**para comprar lembranças** _puh•ruh kaum•<u>prahr</u> leng•<u>bruhn</u>•suhz_

to use the restrooms [toilets]	**para usar os banheiros** *puh•ruh oo•zahr ooz buh•nyay•rooz*	
Is there access for the disabled?	**Há algum acesso para os deficientes?** *ah ahl•goong uh•seh•soo puh•ruh ooz deh•fee•see•ehntz*	

For Tickets, see page 20.

Seeing the Sights

Where is/are...?	**Onde é/são...?** *aund eh/sohm...*
the battleground	**o campo de batalha** *oo kuhm•poo deh buh•tah•lyuh*
the botanical garden	**o jardim botânico** *oo zsuhr•deeng boo•tuh•nee•koo*
the castle	**o castelo** *oo kuhz•teh•loo*
the downtown area	**o centro da cidade** *oo sehn•troo duh see•dahd*
the fountain	**a fonte** *uh faun•teh*
the library	**a biblioteca** *uh bee•blee•aw•teh•kuh*
the market	**o mercado** *oo mehr•kah•doo*
the museum	**o museu** *oo moo•zehoo*
the old town	**a parte velha da cidade** *uh pahrt veh•lyuh duh see•dahd*
the palace	**o palácio** *oo puh•lah•see•yoo*
the park	**o parque** *oo pahr•keh*
the ruins	**as ruínas** *uhz roo•een•uhz*
the shopping area	**a área comercial** *uh ah•ree•uh koo•mehr•see•ahl*
the town square	**a praça central** *uh prah•suh sehn•trahl*
Can you show me on the map?	**Pode indicar no mapa?** *pawd een•dee•kahr noo mah•puh*
It's...	**É...** *eh...*
amazing	**espantoso** *ee•spuhn•tau•zoo*
beautiful	**lindo** *leen•doo*
boring	**aborrecido** *uh•boo•rreh•see•thoo*

interesting	**interessante** _een·teh·reh·<u>suhnt</u>_
magnificent	**magnífico** _mahg·<u>nee</u>·fee·koo_
romantic	**romântico** _roo·<u>muhn</u>·tee·koo_
strange	**estranho** _ee·<u>struh</u>·nyoo_
stunning	**estupendo** _ee·stoo·<u>pehn</u>·doo_
terrible	**horrível** _aw·<u>rree</u>·vehl_
ugly	**feio** _<u>fay</u>·oo_
I (don't) like any of it.	**(Não) gosto de tudo.** _(nohm) <u>gaw</u>·stoo deh <u>too</u>·thoo_

For Asking Directions, see page 36.

Religious Sites

Where's...?	**Onde é...?** _aund eh..._
the cathedral	**a catedral** _uh keh·teh·<u>drahl</u>_
the Catholic/	**a igreja católica/protestante** _uh ee·<u>gray</u>·zsuh_
Protestant church	_kuh·<u>taw</u>·lee·kuh/praw·tee·<u>stuhnt</u>_
the mosque	**a mesquita** _uh mehz·<u>kee</u>·tuh_
Where's...?	**Onde é...?** _aund eh..._
the shrine	**o relicário** _oo reh·lee·<u>kah</u>·ree·oo_
the synagogue	**a sinagoga** _uh seen·uh·<u>gaw</u>·guh_
the temple	**o templo** _oo <u>tehm</u>·ploo_
What time is mass/	**A que horas é a missa/o culto?** _uh kee <u>aw</u>·ruhz eh_
the service?	_uh <u>mee</u>·suh/oo <u>kool</u>·too_

Shopping

ESSENTIAL

Where is the market/mall [shopping?	**Onde é o mercado/o centro comercial?** *aund eh oo mehr•kah•thoo/oo sehn•troo koo•mehr•see•ahl*
I'm just looking.	**Estou só vendo.** *ee•stawoo saw vehn•doo*
Can you help me?	**Pode me ajudar?** *pawd meh uh•zsoo•dahr*
I'm being helped.	**Alguém está me ajudando.** *ahl•gehng ee•stah uh meh uh•zsoo•dahd•doh*
How much is it?	**Quanto é?** *kwuhn•too eh*
That one, please.	**Aquele m /Aquela f, por favor.** *uh•kehl/uh•keh•luh poor fuh•vaur*
That's all, thanks.	**Étudo, obrigado m /obrigada f.** *eh too•doo aw•bree•gah•doo/aw•bree•gah•thuh*
Where can I pay?	**Onde pago?** *aund pah•goo*
I'll pay in cash/by credit card.	**Pago com dinheiro/com o cartão de crédito.** *pah•goo kaum dee•nyay•roo/kaum oo kuhr•tohm deh kreh•dee•too*
A receipt, please.	**Um recibo, por favor.** *oong reh•see•boo poor fuh•vaur*

Some particularly good, value-for-money items to look out for in Brazil include: gemstones and jewelry, leather goods such as sandals, bags, belts and wallets, wooden objects such as salad bowls and trays and woodcarvings, Brazilian percussion instruments and music, lace and embroidery or beachware, religious articles and of course, coffee.

At the Shops

Where is/are...?	**Onde é/são...?** *aund eh/sohm...*
the antiques store	**a loja das antiguidades** *uh law·zsuh duhz uhn·tee·gee·dah·dehz*
the bakery	**a padaria** *uh pah·deh·ree·uh*
the bank	**o banco** *oo buhn·koo*
the bookstore	**a livraria** *uh lee·vreh·ree·uh*
the clothing store	**a loja de artigos de vestuário** *uh law·zsuh deh uhr·tee·gooz de veh·stoo·ah·ree·oo*
the delicatessen	**a loja de conveniência** *uh law·zsuh deh kohn·vuh·nee·uhn·see·ah*
the department store	**a loja de departamentos** *uh law·zsuh deh deh·puhr·tuh·mehn·tooz*
the gift shop	**a loja de recordações** *uh law·zsuh deh reh·kaur·duh·soingz*
the health food store	**a loja de produtos dietéticos** *uh law·zsuh deh proo·doo·tooz dee·eh·tee·kooz*
the jeweler	**a joalheria** *uh zsoo·uh·lyeh·ree·uh*
the liquor store [off-licence]	**a loja de vinhos** *uh law·zsuh deh vee·nyooz*
the market	**o mercado** *oo mehr·kah·doo*
the music store	**a loja de música** *uh law·zsuh deh moo·zee·cuh*
Where is/are...?	**Onde é/são...?** *aund eh/sohm...*
the pastry shop	**a confeitaria** *uh kaun·fay·tuh·ree·uh*
the pharmacy [chemist]	**a farmácia** *uh fuhr·mah·see·uh*
the produce [grocery] store	**a quitanda** *uh kee·tuhn·duh*
the shoe store	**a sapataria** *uh suh·puh·tuh·ree·uh*
the shopping mall [shopping centre]	**o centro comercial** *oo sehn·troo koo·mehr·see·ahl*

the souvenir store	**a loja de lembranças** uh _law_•zsuh deh lehn•_bruhn_•suhz
the supermarket	**o supermercado** oo soo•pehr•mehr•_kah_•thoo
the tobacconist	**a tabacaria** uh tuh•bah•kuh•_ree_•uh
the toy store	**a loja de brinquedos** uh _law_•zsuh deh breeng•_keh_•dooz

Ask an Assistant

What are the opening hours?	**Qual a hora de abertura?** kwahl uh _aw_•ruh deh ah•behr•_too_•ruh
Where is/are…?	**Onde é/são…?** aund eh/sohm…
the cashier	**a caixa** uh _keye_•shuh
the escalator	**a escada rolante** uh ees•_kah_•duh roo•_luhnt_
the elevator [lift]	**o elevador** oo eh•leh•vuh•_daur_
the fitting room	**os vestiários** ooz vehs•tee•_ah_•ree•ooz
the store directory [guide]	**a planta da loja** uh _pluhn_•tuh duh _law_•zsuh
Can you help me?	**Pode me ajudar?** pawd meh uh•zsoo•_dahr_
I'm just looking.	**Estou só vendo.** ee•_stawoo_ saw _vehn_•doo
I'm being helped.	**Alguém está a me ajudar.** ahl•_geng_ ee•_stah_ uh meh uh•zsoo•_dahr_
Do you have…?	**Tem…?** teng…

Could you show me...? **Pode me mostrar...?** *poo•dee meh mooz•trahr...*

Can you ship it /wrap it ? **Pode despachá-lo/embrulhá-lo?** *pawd dehs•puh•shah•loo/eng•broo•lyah•loo*

How much is it? **Quanto é?** *kwuhn•too eh*

That's all, thanks. **É tudo, obrigado m /obrigada f.** *eh too•doo aw•bree•gah•doo/aw•bree•gah•duh*

For Clothing, see page 127.

YOU MAY HEAR...

Deseja alguma coisa? *deh•zay•zuh ahl•goo•muh koy•zuh* — Would you like something?

Um momento. *oong moo•mehn•too* — One moment.

O que é que deseja? *oo kee eh keh deh•zay•zsuh* — What would you like?

Mais alguma coisa? *meyez ahl•goo•muh koy•zuh* — Anything else?

YOU MAY SEE...

HORÁRIO DE ABERTURA	opening hours
FECHADO PARA ALMOÇO	closed for lunch
PROVADOR	fitting room
CAIXA	cashier
SÓ DINHEIRO	cash only
CARTÕES DE CRÉDITO ACEITES	credit cards accepted

Personal Preferences

I'd like something...	**Queria uma coisa...** keh•_ree_•uh _oo_•muh koy•zuh...
cheap/expensive	**barata/cara** buh•_rah_•tuh/_kah_•ruh
larger/smaller	**maior/menor** meye•_awr_/_mee_•nawr
from this region	**desta região** _dehs_•tuh ree•zsee•_ohm_
Around... reais.	**Cerca de... reais.** sehr•ka deh... rree•_eyez_
Is it real?	**É verdadeiro?** eh vehr•duh•_day_•roo
Could you show me this/that ?	**Podia mostrar-me este/esse?** poo•_dee_•uh moos•_trahr_•meh ehst/ehs
That's not quite what I want.	**Não é bem o que quero.** nohm eh beng oo keh _keh_•roo
No, I don't like it.	**Não, não gosto.** nohm nohm _gaw_•stoo
It's too expensive.	**É caro demais.** eh _kah_•roo deh•_meyez_
I have to think about it.	**Tenho que pensar nisto.** _tay_•nyoo keh pehn•_sahr_ _nee_•stoo
I'll take it.	**Levo.** _leh_•voo

For Souvenirs see page 133.

Paying & Bargaining

How much?	**Quanto é?** _kwuhn_•too eh
I'll pay...	**Pago...** _pah_•goo...
in cash	**com dinheiro** kaum dee•_nyay_•roo
by credit card	**com o cartão de crédito** kaum oo kuhr•_tohm_ deh _kreh_•dee•too
by traveler's check [cheque]	**com cheque** kaum _sheh_•keh
A receipt, please.	**Um recibo, por favor.** oong reh•_see_•boo poor fuh•_vaur_
That's too much.	**Isso é muito.** _ee_•soo eh _mooee_•too
I'll give you...	**Vou dar-lhe...** vau _dahr_•lyeh...
I only have... reais.	**Só tenho...reais.** saw _teh_•nyoo...rree•_eyez_

| Is that your best price? | **É o preço melhor que me pode dar?** *eh oo* *preh•soo mee•lyawr keh meh pawd dahr* |
| Can you give me a discount? | **Pode-me dar um desconto?** *pawd•meh dahr oong* *dehs•kaun•too* |

For Numbers, see page 173.

International credit cards are generally accepted. The most commonly used cards are Visa™, American Express®, Europay/ Mastercard™, JCB and Maestro®. In some small villages and towns cash may still be the only form of currency accepted.

YOU MAY HEAR...

Como deseja pagar? *kau•moo deh•zay•zsuh puh•gahr*	How are you paying?
Esta transação não foi autorizada. *eh•stuh truhn•suh•sohm nohm foy ahoo•too•ree•zah•thuh*	This transaction was not authorized.
Não aceitamos cartões de crédito. *nohm uh•say•tuh•mooz kuhr•toings deh kreh•dee•too*	We don't accept credit cards.
Só com dinheiro, por favor. *saw kaum dee•nyay•roo poor fuh•vaur*	Cash only, please.
Não tem troco [trocado]? *nohm teng trau•koo [trau•kah•doo]*	Do you have any smaller bills?
A identificação, por favor. *uh ee•dehnt•tee•fee•kuh•sohm, poor fuh•vaur*	ID, please.

Making a Complaint

I'd like...	**Queria...** keh•<u>ree</u>•uh...
to exchange this	**trocar isto** troo•<u>kahr</u> ee•stoo
to return this	**retornar isto** ree•tawrr•<u>nahr</u> ee•stoo
a refund	**um reembolso** oong ree•eng•<u>baul</u>•soo
to see the manager	**falar com o gerente** *m* /**a gerente** *f* fuh•<u>lahr</u> kaum oo zseh•<u>rehnt</u>/uh zseh•<u>rehnt</u>

Services

Can you recommend...?	**Pode recomendar...?** pawd reh•koo•mehn•<u>dahr</u>...
a barber	**o cabeleireiro de homens** oo kuh•beh•lay•<u>ray</u>•roo deh <u>aw</u>•mengs
a dry cleaner	**a lavandaria de limpeza a seco** uh luh•vuhn•duh•<u>ree</u>•uh deh leeng•<u>peh</u>•zuh uh <u>seh</u>•koo
a hairdresser	**o cabeleireiro de senhoras** oo kuh•beh•lay•<u>ray</u>•roo deh see•<u>nyau</u>•ruhz
a laundromat [launderette]	**lavanderia** uh luh•vuhn•deh•<u>ree</u>•uh
a nail salon	**o salão de unhas** oo suh•<u>lohm</u> deh <u>oo</u>•nyuhz
a spa	**o spa** oo spa
a travel agency	**a agência de viagens** uh ah•<u>zsehn</u>•see•uh deh vee•<u>ah</u>•zsengs

Can you…this?	**Pode…isto?** *pawd…ee•stoo*	
alter	**modificar** *moo•dee•fee•kahr*	
clean	**limpar** *leem•pahr*	
mend	**consertar** *kaun•sehr•tahr*	
press	**engomar** *eeng•goo•mahr*	
When will it be ready?	**Quando estará pronto?** *kwuhn•doo ee•stuh•rah praun•too*	

Hair & Beauty

I'd like…	**Queria…** *keh•ree•uh…*
an appointment for today/tomorrow	**marcar um horário para hoje/amanhã** *muhr•kahr oong aw•rah•ree•oo puh•ruh auzseh/uh•muh•nyuh*
some color	**alguma cor** *ahl•goo•muh kaur*
some highlights	**madeixas** *muh•day•shuhz*
my hair styled/ blow-dried	**meu cabelo penteado/seco com secador** *mehoo kuh•beh•loo pehn•tee•ah•thoo/seh•koo kaum seh•kuh•daur*
a haircut	**um corte** *oong kawrt*
a trim	**acertar as pontas [aparar]** *uh•sehr•tahr uhz paun•tuhz [uh•puh•rahr]*
Don't cut it too short.	**Não corte muito curto.** *nohm kawrt mooee•too koor•too*
Shorter here.	**Mais curto aqui.** *meyez koor•too uh•kee*
I'd like…	**Queria…** *keh•ree•uh…*
an eyebrow/ a bikini wax	**depilar as sombrancelhas/depilar para biquini** *duh•pee•lahr oo•muh seh•ruh deh sau•bruhn•seh•lyuhz/par•ah bee•kee•nee*
I'd like…	**Queria…** *keh•ree•uh…*
a facial	**uma limpeza de pele** *oo•muh leem•peh•zuh deh pehl*

a manicure/pedicure	**fazer as unhas das mãos/pés**	*faz•uhr uhz oo•nyaz duhz muh•oonz/pehz*
a (sports) massage	**uma massagem (esportiva)**	*oo•muh mehn•sah•zseng (ee•spawr•tee•vuh)*
Do you do...?	**Faz...?**	*fahz...*
acupuncture	**acupuntura**	*uh•koo•poon•too•ruh*
aromatherapy	**aromaterapia**	*uh•raw•muh•teh•reh•pee•uh*
oxygen treatment	**tratamento de oxigênio**	*truh•tuh•mehn•too deh awk•see•zseh•nee•oo*
Is there a sauna?	**Há sauna?**	*ah sahoo•nuh*

Check with your hotel concierge for information on local spas that offer massage, acupuncture and skin treatments. These spas are most often found in large cities. The service fee is usually included in the price, but an additional 10% tip is appreciated for good service.

Antiques

How old is this?	**Qual é a data disto?**	*kwahl eh uh dah•tuh dee•stoo*
Do you have anything from the...period?	**Tem alguma coisa do período...?**	*teng ahl•goo•muh koy•zuh thoo peh•ree•oo•thoo...*
Do I have to fill out any forms?	**Tenho que completar algum formulário?**	*teh•nyoo keh kaum•pleh•tahr ahl•goom fawr•moo•lah•ree•oo*
Is there a certificate of authenticity?	**Há um certificado de autenticidade?**	*ah oong sehr•tee•fee•kah•thoo deh aw•tehn•tee•see•dahd*
Can you ship/wrap it?	**Pode enviar/embrulhar?**	*pawd ehn•vee•ahr/ehm•broo•lyahr*

Clothing

I'd like...	**Queria...** *keh•ree•uh...*
Can I try this on?	**Posso provar isto?** *paw•soo proo•vahr ee•stoo*
It doesn't fit.	**Não me serve.** *nohm meh sehrv*
It's too...	**É muito...** *eh mooee•too...*
big	**grande** *grawnd*
small	**pequeno m /pequena f** *peh•kehn•oo/peh•kehn•uh*
short	**curto m /curta f** *koor•too/koor•tuh*
long	**comprido m /comprida f** *kaum•pree•doo/ kaum•pree•duh*
tight/loose	**justo/largo** *zsooz•too/lahr•goo*
Do you have this in size...?	**Tem isto no tamanho...?** *teng ee•stoo noo tuh•muh•nyoo...*
Do you have this in a bigger/smaller size?	**Tem isto num tamanho maior/menor?** *teng ee•stoo noong tuh•muh•nyoo meye•awr/mee•nor*

For Numbers, see page 173.

YOU MAY HEAR...

Isso fica bem em você. *ee•soo fee•kuh beng eng voh•seh*	That looks great on you.
Como é que fica? *kau•moo eh keh fee•kuh*	How does it fit?
Não temos o seu tamanho. *nohm teh•mooz oo sehoo tuh•muh•nyoo*	We don't have your size.

YOU MAY SEE...

ROUPA DE HOMEM	men's clothing
ROUPA DE SENHORA	women's clothing
ROUPA DE CRIANÇAS	children's clothing

Colors

I'd like something...	**Queria algo...**	*keh•ree•uh ahl•goo...*
beige	**em bege**	*eng bay•zseh*
black	**em preto**	*eng preh•too*
blue	**em azul**	*eng uh•zool*
brown	**em marrom**	*muh•rraum*
green	**em verde**	*eng vehrd*
gray	**em cinza**	*eng seen•zuh*
orange	**em laranja**	*eng luh•ruhn•zsuh*
pink	**em cor-de-rosa**	*eng kaur deh raw•zuh*
purple	**em roxo**	*eng rau•shoo*
red	**em vermelho**	*eng vehr•meh•lyoo*
white	**em branco**	*eng bruhn•koo*
yellow	**em amarelo**	*eng uh•meh•reh•loo*

Clothes & Accessories

backpack	**a mochila**	*uh moo•shee•luh*
belt	**o cinto**	*oo seen•too*
bikini	**o bikini [biquini]**	*oo bee•kee•nee [bee•kee•nee]*
blouse	**a blusa**	*uh bloo•zuh*
bra	**o sutiã**	*oo soo•tee•uh*
briefs [underpants]	**as calcinhas**	*uhz kahl•see•nyuhz*
coat	**o casaco comprido**	*oo kuh•zah•koo kaum•pree•thoo*
dress	**o vestido**	*oo vehs•tee•thoo*
hat	**o chapéu**	*oo shuh•pehoo*
jacket	**o casaco curto**	*oo kuh•zah•koo koor•too*
jeans	**as calças jeans**	*uhz kahl•suhz jeans*
pants [trousers]	**as calças**	*uhz kahl•suhz*
pantyhose [tights]	**o collant**	*oo koo•luhnt*
purse [handbag]	**a mala de mão [bolsa]**	

	uh mah•luh deh mohm [baul•sah]	
raincoat	**capa de chuva** *cah•pah deh shoo•vah*	
scarf	**o lenço de pescoço**	
	oo lehn•soo deh pehz•kau•soo	
shirt	**a camisa** *uh kuh•mee•zuh*	
shorts	**os shorts** *ooz shortz*	
skirt	**a saia** *uh seye•uh*	
socks	**as meias curtas** *uhz may•uhz koor•tuhz*	
suit	**o terno** *oo tehr•noo*	
sunglasses	**os óculos de sol** *ooz aw•koo•looz deh sawl*	
sweater	**o suéter** *oo sweh•tur*	
sweatshirt	**o sweatshirt** *oo sweht•shurt [uh bloo•zuh deh mool•ee•tawn]*	
swimming trunks	**os shorts de banho** *ooz shortz deh buh•nyoo*	
swimsuit	**o maiô** *oo meye•au*	
T-shirt	**a camiseta/T-shirt** *uh kuh•mee•seh•tuh/tee•shurt*	
tie	**gravata** *gruh•vah•tuh*	
underwear	**roupa de baixo** *rau•puh deh bah•ee•shoo*	

Fabric

I'd like...	**Queria...** *keh•ree•uh...*	
cotton	**algodão** *ahl•goo•dohm*	
denim	**jeans** *jeanz*	
lace	**renda** *rehn•duh*	
leather	**couro** *kau•roo*	
linen	**linho** *lee•nyoo*	
silk	**seda** *seh•thuh*	
wool	**lã** *luh*	
Is it machine washable?	**Isto é para lavar na máquina?**	
	ee•stoo eh puh•ruh luh•vahr nuh mah•kee•nuh	

Shoes

I'd like a pair of...	**Queria um par de...** keh•*ree*•uh oong pahr deh...
high-heeled/ flat shoes	**sapatos altos/baixos** suh•*pah*•tooz *ahl*•tooz/ *beye*•shooz
boots	**botas** *baw*•tuhz
loafers	**loafers** *loa*•ferz
sandals	**sandálias** suhn•*dah*•lee•uhz
shoes	**sapatos** suh•*pah*•tooz
slippers	**chinelas** shee•*neh*•luhz
sneakers	**tênis** *tehn*•ehz
In size...	**No tamanho...** noo tuh•*muh*•nyoo...

For Numbers, see page 173.

Sizes

small (S)	**pequeno** peh•*keh*•noo
medium (M)	**médio** *meh*•dee•oo
large (L)	**grande** gruhnd
extra large (XL)	**extra grande** *ay*•struh gruhnd
petite	**pequeno** peh•*keh*•noo
plus size	**tamanho de factor positivo** tuh•*muh*•nyoo deh *fah*•taur poo•see•*tee*•voo

Newsagent & Tobacconist

Do you sell English-language newspapers?	**Vende jornais em inglês?** _vehn•deh zsoor•neyez eng eeng•lehz_
I'd like...	**Queria...** _keh•ree•uh..._
candy [sweets]	**balas** _bah•luhz_
chewing gum	**goma de mascar** _gau•muh deh muhz•kahr_
a chocolate bar	**uma barra de chocolate** _oonga bar•rah deh shoo•koo•lah•teh_
a cigar	**um charuto** _oong shuh•roo•too_
I'd like...	**Queria...** _keh•ree•uh..._
a pack/carton of cigarettes	**um maço/pacote de cigarros** _oong mah•soo/puh•kaut deh see•gah•rrooz_
a lighter	**um isqueiro** _oong ees•kay•roo_
a magazine	**uma revista** _oo•muh reh•vee•stuh_
matches	**fósforos** _fawz•fuh•rooz_
a newspaper	**um jornal** _oong zsoorr•nahl_
a pen	**uma caneta** _oo•muh kuh•neh•tuh_
a postcard	**um postal** _oong poo•stahl_
a road/town map of...	**um mapa de/da cidade de...** _oong mah•puh deh/deh see•dahd deh..._
stamps	**selos** _seh•looz_

Photography

I'm looking for…camera.	**Estou à procura de [procurando] uma máquina fotográfica…** *ee•stawoo ah praw•koo•ruh deh [praw•koo•ruhn•doo] oo•muh mah•kee•nuh faw•too•grah•fee•kuh…*	
an automatic	**automática** *ahoo•too•mah•tee•kuh*	
a digital	**digital** *deh•zseh•tahl*	
a disposable	**descartável** *dehz•kuhr•tah•vehl*	
I'd like…	**Queria…** *keh•ree•uh…*	
a battery	**uma pilha** *oo•muh pee•lyuh*	
digital prints	**impressões digitais** *eem•preh•soingz deh•zseh•teyez*	
a memory card	**um cartão de memória** *oong kuhr•tohm deh meh•maw•ree•uh*	
Can I print digital photos here?	**Posso imprimir fotos digitais aqui?** *paw•soo eem•pree•meer faw•tooz deh•zeh•teyez uh•kee*	

Souvenirs

bottle of wine	**a garrafa de vinho** *uh guh•rrah•fuh deh vee•nyoo*
box of chocolates	**a caixa de chocolates** *uh keye•shuh deh shoo•koo•lah•tehz*
calendar	**o calendário** *oo kuh•lehn•dah•ree•oo*
postcards	**postais** *pooz•teyez*
scarf	**o lenço** *oo lehn•soo*
souvenir guide	**o guia turístico** *oo gee•uh too•ree•stee•koo*
T-shirt	**a camiseta** *uh kuh•mee•seh•tuh*
toy/game	**o brinquedo/jogo** *oo breeng•keh•thoo/zsaw•goo*
wine	**o vinho** *oo vee•nyoo*
Can I see this/that?	**Posso ver este/esse?** *paw•soo vehr ehst/eh•seh*
It's the one in the window/display case.	**É aquele na janela/vitrine.** *eh uh•kehl nuh zsuh•neh•luh/vee•treen*

I'd like...	**Queria...** *keh·ree·uh...*
a battery	**uma pilha** <u>oo</u>·muh <u>pee</u>·lyuh
a bracelet	**uma pulseira** <u>oo</u>·muh pool·<u>say</u>·ruh
a brooch	**um broche** oong brawsh
earrings	**brincos** <u>breeng</u>·kooz
a necklace	**um colar** oong koo·<u>lahr</u>
a ring	**um anel** oong uh·<u>nehl</u>
a watch	**um relógio de pulso** oong reh·<u>loy</u>·zsoo deh <u>pool</u>·soo
copper	**cobre** <u>kaw</u>·breh
crystal	**cristal** kree·<u>stahl</u>
diamonds	**brilhantes** bree·<u>lyuhntz</u>
white/yellow gold	**ouro branco/amarelo** <u>au</u>·roo <u>bruhn</u>·koo/ uh·muh·<u>reh</u>·loo
pearls	**pérolas** <u>peh</u>·roo·luhz
pewter	**peltre** <u>pehl</u>·treh
platinum	**platina** <u>plah</u>·tee·nuh
sterling silver	**prata** <u>prah</u>·tuh
Is this real?	**É verdadeiro?** eh vehr·duh·<u>day</u>·roo
Can you engrave it?	**Pode gravá-lo?** pawd gruh·<u>vah</u>·loo

---

Ceramics such as clay bowls and water jugs are a particulary good purchase in the northeast, as well as clay figurines depicting folk heroes, customs and celebrations, and handmade lace and embroidered clothing. From the Amazon, look for Marajoara ceramic pieces decorated with geometric patterns. Straw and natural fibre baskets, hats, bags mats, etc. are all popular souvenirs too.

Afro-Brazilian musical instruments provide alternative ideas as presents. Some examples are **berimbau** (a stretched metal strip, played with a stick), **bongô** (bongo drums) and **atabaque** (another type of drum).

ESSENTIAL

When's the game?	**Quando é o jogo?** _kwuhn•doo eh o zsau•goo_
Where's…?	**Onde é…?** _aund eh…_
the beach	**a praia** _uh preye•uh_
the park	**o parque** _oo pahr•keh_
the pool	**a piscina** _uh pee•see•nuh_
Is it safe to swim here?	**Pode nadar aqui sem perigo?** _pawd nuh•dahr uh•kee sehn peh•ree•goo_
Can I hire golf clubs?	**Posso alugar tacos?** _paw•soo uh•loo•gahr tah•kooz_
How much per hour?	**Qual é a tarifa por hora?** _kwahl eh uh tuh•ree•fuh poor aw•ruh_
How far is it to…?	**A que distância fica…?** _uh keh dee•stuhn•see•uh fee•kuh…_
Can you show me on the map?	**Pode indicar no mapa?** _pawd een•dee•kahr noo mah•puh_

Watching Sport

When's…?	**Quando é…?** _kwuhn•doo eh…_
the basketball game	**o jogo de basquetebol** _oo zsau•goo deh bah•skeht•bawl_
the boxing match	**a partida de boxe** _uh puhr•tee•duh deh bawkz_
the cycling race	**a corrida de bicicleta** _uh koo•ree•thuh deh bee•see•kleht_
the golf tournament	**o torneio de golfe** _oo taur•nay•oo deh gawlf_
the soccer [football] game	**o jogo de futebol** _oo zsau•goo deh foo•teh•bawl_

Brazilians are avid soccer fans and the sport unites all ages and classes. Rio boasts Maracanã, the largest soccer stadium in the world. Be warned, during World Cup season, the country grinds to a halt!

When's...?	**Quando é...?** _kwuhn•doo eh..._
the basketball game	**o jogo de basquete** _oo zsau•goo deh bah•skeht_
the tennis match	**a partida de tênis** _uh puhr•tee•thuh de teh•neez_
the volleyball game	**o jogo de vôlei** _oo zsau•goo deh vaw•lay_
Which teams are playing?	**Quais são os times que jogam?** _kweyez sohm ooz tee•mehs keh zsau•gohm_
Where's...?	**Onde é...?** _aund eh..._
the horsetrack	**a pista de cavalo** _uh peez•tuh deh kuh•vah•loo_
the racetrack	**o hipódromo** _oo ee•paw•drau•moo_
the stadium	**o estádio** _oo uhs•tah•dee•oo_
Where can I place a bet?	**Onde posso fazer uma aposta?** _aund paw•soo fah•zaer uh•paws•tuh_

Playing Sport

Where's...?	**Onde é...?** _aund eh..._
the golf course	**o campo de golfe** _oo kuhm•poo deh gawlf_

the gym	**o clube desportivo [esportivo]** _oo kloob dehs•poor•tee•voo [ees•poor•tee•voo]_
the park	**o parque** _oo pahrk_
the tennis courts	**os campos [as quadras] de tênis** _ooz kuhm•pooz [uhz kwah•druhz] deh teh•neez_
How much per...?	**Qual é o preço por...?** _kwahl eh oo preh•soo poor..._
day	**dia** _dee•uh_
hour	**hora** _aw•ruh_
game	**jogo** _zsau•goo_
round	**volta** _vawl•tuh_
Can I rent [hire]...?	**Posso alugar...?** _paw•soo uh•loo•gahr..._
golf clubs	**tacos de golfe** _tah•kooz deh gawlf_
equipment	**o equipamento** _oo ee•kee•puh•mehn•too_
a racket	**uma raquete** _oo•muh rah•keht_

At the Beach/Pool

Where's the beach/pool?	**Onde é a praia/piscina?** _aund eh uh preye•uh/pee•see•nuh_
Is there...?	**Há...?** _ah..._
a kiddie pool	**uma piscina para crianças** _oo•muh pee•see•nuh puh•ruh kree•uhn•suhs_
an indoor/outdoor pool	**uma piscina coberta/ao ar livre** _oo•muh pee•see•nuh koo•behr•tuh/ahoo ahr lee•vreh_
a lifeguard	**uma salva-vidas** _oo•muh sahl•vuh vee•duhz_
Is it safe...?	**É perigoso...?** _eh per•ree•gau•zoo..._
to swim	**para nadar** _puh•ruh nuh•dahr_
to dive	**para mergulhar** _puh•ruh mehr•goo•lyahr_
for children	**para as crianças** _puh•ruh uhz kree•uhn•suhs_
I want to hire...	**Quero alugar...** _keh•roo uh•loo•gahr..._
a deck chair	**uma cadeira de encosto** _oo•muh kuh•day•ruh deh ehn•kaus•stoo_

diving equipment	**equipamento para mergulhar**
	ee•kee•puh•<u>mehn</u>•too <u>puh</u>•ruh mehr•goo•<u>lyahr</u>
a jet-ski	**um jet-ski** *oong <u>zseht</u>•skee*
a motorboat	**um barco a motor** *oong <u>bahr</u>•koo uh moo•<u>taur</u>*
a rowboat	**um barco a remos** *oong <u>bahr</u>•koo uh <u>reh</u>•mooz*
snorkling equipment	**equipamento de snorkling** *ee•kee•puh•<u>mehn</u>•too de <u>snawr</u>•kleeng*
a surfboard	**uma prancha de surf** <u>oo</u>•muh <u>pruhn</u>•shuh deh soorf
a towel	**uma toalha** <u>oo</u>•muh too•<u>ah</u>•lyuh
an umbrella	**um guarda sol** *oong <u>gwahr</u>•duh sawl*
water skis	**esquis-aquáticos** *eez•<u>keez</u> uh•<u>kwah</u>•tee•kooz*
a windsurfer	**uma prancha à vela** <u>oo</u>•muh <u>pruhn</u>•shuh ah <u>veh</u>•luh
For…hours.	**Por…horas.** *poor…<u>aw</u>•ruhz*

Brazil is practically synonymous with long stretches of golden beaches; **Copacabana** and **Ipanema** in Rio are known the world over. Surfing is popular all along the Brazilian coast, and beach volleyball is also a popular pursuit. The largest beaches have lifeguards, but look for the following swimming flags: red (swimming forbidden), yellow (swim near the beach), green (safe).

Brazil and its beaches are equally synonymous with tiny bikinis. The local **tanga** (string bikini) or **fio dental** (literally "dental floss") can be purchased everywhere, and many stores are solely dedicated to swimwear. Despite this however, don't forget that Brazil is a deeply Catholic and often conservative country. Topless sunbathing is regarded as offensive.

Out in the Country

I'd like a map…	**Queria um mapa…** keh·_ree_·uh oong _mah_·puh…
of this region	**desta região** _deh_·stuh reh·zsee·_ohm_
of the walking routes	**de roteiros a pé** deh roh·_tay_·rooz a peh
of bike routes	**de roteiros de bicicleta** deh roh·_tay_·rooz deh bee·see·_kleh_·tuh
of the trails	**dos caminhos** thooz kuh·_mee_·nyooz
Is it easy/difficult?	**É fácil/difícil?** eh _fah_·seel/dee·_fee_·seel
Is it far/steep?	**É distante/íngreme?** eh deez·_tuhnt_/een·grae·meh
How far is it to…?	**A que distância fica…** uh keh dee·_stuhn_·see·uh _fee_·kuh…
Can you show me on the map?	**Pode indicar no mapa?** pawd een·dee·_kahr_ noo _mah_·puh
I'm lost.	**Estou perdido m /perdida f.** ee·_stawoo_ pehr·_dee_·doo/pehr·_dee_·duh
Where's…?	**Onde é…?** aund eh…
the bridge	**a ponte** uh paunt
the cave	**a caverna** uh kuh·_vehr_·nuh
the cliff	**a falésia** uh fuh·_leh_·see·uh
the desert	**o deserto** oo deh·_zehr_·too
the farm	**a fazenda** uh fuh·_zehn_·dah

the field	**o campo**
	oo <u>kuhm</u>•poo
the forest	**a floresta**
	uh flau•<u>reh</u>•stuh
the hill	**a colina** *uh koo•<u>lee</u>•nuh*
the lake	**o lago** *oo <u>lah</u>•goo*
the mountain	**a montanha** *uh maun•<u>tah</u>•nyuh*
the nature preserve	**a reserva natural**
	uh reh•<u>zehr</u>•vuh nuh•too•<u>rahl</u>
the view point	**o mirante** *oo mee•ruhnt*
the park	**o parque** *oo pahrk*
the path	**o caminho para pedestres**
	oo kuh•<u>mee</u>•nyoo <u>puh</u>•ruh peh•<u>dehs</u>•trehz
the peak	**o pico** *oo <u>pee</u>•koo*
the picnic area	**a área de piqueniques**
	a ahr•ee•uh deh pee•keh•nee•kehz
the pond	**a lagoa**
	uh luh•<u>gaw</u>•uh
the river	**o rio** *oo <u>rree</u>•oo*
the sea	**o mar** *oo mahr*
the valley	**o vale** *oo vahl*

Where's...?	**Onde é...?** *aund eh...*
the vineyard	**o vinhedo** *uh vee•nyeh•doo*
the waterfall	**a cachoeira**
	uh kuh•shway•ra
I want to hire...	**Quero alugar...**
	eh•roo uh•loo•gahr...
boots	**botas**
	baw•tuhz
a helmet	**um capacete**
	oong kuh•puh•seht
These are too big/small.	**Estes são muito grandes/pequenos.**
	ehs•tehz sohm mooee•too gruhn•dehz/pee•keh•nooz
Are there lessons?	**Tem aulas?** *Teng ahoo•laz*
I'm a beginner.	**Sou principiante.**
	sawoo preen•see•puhnt
I'm experienced.	**Tenho experiência.**
	teh•nyoo ees•peh•ree•ehn•see•uh
A trail [piste] map, please.	**Um mapa da trilha, por favor.**
	oong mah•puh deh tree•lyuh poor fuh•vaur

YOU MAY SEE...

BONDE/FUNICULAR	cable car/gondola
TELEFÉRICO	chair lift
INICIANTE	novice
INTERMEDIÁRIO	intermediate
AVANÇADO	expert
PISTA FECHADA	trail [piste] closed

Going Out

ESSENTIAL

What is there to do in the evenings?	**O que há para se fazer à noite?** *oo keh ah puh•ruh seh fuh•zehr ah noyt*
Do you have a program of events?	**Tem um programa dos espectáculos?** *teng oong proo•gruh•muh dooz ee•spehk•tah•koo•looz*
What's playing at the movies [cinema] tonight?	**O que está passando no cinema hoje à noite?** *oo kee ee•stah pah•san•doh noo see•neh•muh auzseh ah noyt*
Where's...?	**Onde é...?** *aund eh...*
the downtown area	**o centro** *oo sehn•troo*
the bar	**o bar** *oo bar*
the dance club	**a discoteca** *uh deez•koo•teh•kuh*
Is there a cover charge?	**É preciso pagar entrada [ingresso]?** *eh preh•see•zoo puh•gahr ehn•trah•duh [een•greh•soo]*

Entertainment

Can you recommend...?	**Pode recomendar...?** *pawd reh•koo•mehn•dahr...*
a concert	**um concerto** *oong kaun•sehr•too*
a movie	**um filme** *oong feel•meh*
an opera	**uma ópera** *oo•muh aw•peh•ruh*
a play	**uma peça de teatro** *oo•muh peh•ssah duh tee•ah•troo*
When does it start/end?	**A que horas começa/acaba?** *uh kee aw•ruhz koo•meh•suh/uh•kah•buh*
What's the dress code?	**Qual é o traje apropriado?** *Kwal eh oo trahj ah•praw•pree•ah•doo*

I like…	**Gosto de…** _gaws•too deh_…
classical music	**música clássica** _moo•zee•kuh klah•see•kuh_
folk music	**música popular** _moo•zee•kuh poo•poo•lahr_
jazz	**jazz** _zsahz_
pop music	**pop** _pawp_
rap	**rap** _rahp_

For Tickets, see page 20.

Carnaval is widely celebrated in Brazil. A time of lavish celebration before Lent, **Carnaval** begins four days before Ash Wednesday, and ends with the famous 'Fat Tuesday' celebration. Look for parades on the streets and carnival balls (**bailes carnavalescos**). The famed **Carnaval do Rio** sees the spectacularly colorful competition between the various samba schools in a parade through the streets of Rio de Janeiro.

Samba and **bossa nova** are the dance styles best known abroad, but look out for regional rhythms like **pagode**, **lambada**, **frevo**, **forró**, **maracatu**, **baião**, **carimbó** and **bumba-meu boi**, with their mixture of African, Indian, and European influences.

Local papers and weekly entertainment guides such as **Veja** will tell you what's on and have good restaurant listings too. Regional booklets (**vejinha**) are also useful. To purchase tickets online in advance, try www.ingresso.com.br. It is good for movies, shows and theme parks. For sporting events, try www.ingressofacil.com.br. Alternatively, Ticketmaster also sells tickets for shows, concerts and sporting events.

Nightlife

What is there to do in the evenings?	**O que há para se fazer à noite?** *oo keh ah puh•ruh seh fuh•zehr ah noyt*
Can you recommend...?	**Pode recomendar...?** *pawd reh•koo•mehn•dahr...*
a bar	**um bar** *oong bar*
a casino	**um casino** *oong kuh•see•noo*
a dance club	**uma discoteca** *oo•muh dee•skoo•teh•kuh*
a gay club	**um clube gay** *oong kloob gay*
a jazz club	**um clube de jazz** *oong kloob deh zsahz*
a club with Brazilian music?	**uma discoteca com música brasileira?** *oo•muh dee•skoo•teh•kuh kaum moo•zee•kuh bruh•see•lay•ruh*
Is there live music?	**Há música ao vivo?** *ah moo•zee•kuh ahoo vee•voo*
How do I get there?	**Como é que vou até lá?** *kau•moo eh keh vauoo uh•teh lah*
Is there a cover charge?	**É preciso pagar entrada [ingresso]?** *eh preh•see•zoo puh•gahr ehn•trah•duh [een•greh•soo]*

Let's go dancing.	**Vamos dançar.**
	vuh•mooz duhn•sahr
Is this area safe at night?	**Esta área é segura à noite?** _eh•stuh ah•rryah eh seh•goo•ruh ah noyt?_

YOU MAY HEAR...

Desligue os seus celulares, por favor.	Turn off your cell [mobile] phones, please.
dehz•lee•geh oohz sehooz sehl•oo•lahrz poor fuh•vaur	

Special Requirements

ESSENTIAL

I'm here on business.	**Estou aqui a negócios.** *ee·stawoo uh·kee ah neh·gaw·see·oosz*
Here's my business card.	**Tome o meu cartão.** *taw·meh oo meeoo kuhr·tohm*
Can I have your card?	**Por favor, o seu cartão?** *poor fuh·vaur oo sehoo kuhr·tohm*
I have a meeting with...?	**Tenho uma reunião com...** *tay·nyoo oomah rree·oo·nee·ohm kaum...*
Where's...?	**Onde é...** *aund eh...*
the business center	**o centro de negócios** *oo sehn·troo deh neh·gaw·see·oosz*
the convention hall	**a sala de convenção** *ah sah·lah deh kaun·vehn·sohmz*
the meeting room	**a sala de reunião** *ah sah·lah deh rree·oo·nee·ohmz*

On Business

I'm here to attend...	**Estou aqui para participar...** *ee·stawoo uh·kee puh·ruh puhr·tee·see·pahr...*
a seminar	**de um seminário** *deh oong seh·mee·nah·ree·oo*
a conference	**de uma conferência** *deh oomuh kaun·feh·rehn·see·uh*
a meeting	**de uma reunião** *deh oomuh rree·oo·nee·ohm*
My name is...	**Meu nome é...** *mehoo naum·ee eh...*
May I introduce my colleague...	**Posso apresentar o meu colega** *m* /**a minha colega** *f...* *paw·soo uh·preh·zehn·tahr oo mehoo koo·leh·guh/uh mee·nyuh koo·leh·guh...*

First names should normally be used for business dealings, but it is also important to use the person's title. When meeting and greeting, offer a firm handshake and good eye contact. On departure you should repeat the process again. It's best to avoid trying to set up any business meetings around Carneval as everything shuts down at this time.

I have a meeting/ an appointment with...	**Tenho uma reunião com...** _tay·nyoo oo·muh rree·oo·nee·ohm kaum..._
I'm sorry I'm late.	**Desculpe, estou atrasado m /atrasada f.** _dehs·kool·puh ee·stawoo uh·truh·zah·thoo/ uh·truh·zah·thuh_
I need an interpreter.	**Preciso de um tradutor.** _preh·see·zoo deh oong truh·doo·taur_
You can reach me at the...Hotel.	**Pode me encontrar no hotel...** _pawd·eh meh eng·kaun·trahr noo aw·tehl..._
I'm here until...	**Estou aqui até...** _ee·stawoo uh·kee uh·teh..._

I need to...	**Preciso de...** *preh•see•zoo deh...*
make a call	**fazer um telefonema** *fuh•zehr oong teh•leh•faw•neh•muh*
make a photocopy	**fazer uma fotocópia** *fuh•zehr oo•muh faw•taw•kaw•pee•uh*
send an e-mail	**enviar um e-mail** *eng•vee•ahr oong ee•mehl*
send a fax	**enviar um fax** *ehn•vee•ahr oong fahks*
send a package (overnight)	**enviar um embrulho (de um dia para o outro)** *ehn•vee•ahr oong eng•broo•lyoo (deh oong dee•uh puh•ruh oo aw•troo)*
It was a pleasure to meet you.	**Muito prazer.** *mooee•too pruh•zehr*

For Communications, see page 52.

YOU MAY HEAR...

Você tem uma hora marcado?
vaw•seh teng oo•muh oh•rah mahr•cah•doo
Do you have an appointment?

Com quem? *kaum keng*
With whom?

Está numa reunião. *ee•stah noo•muh ree•oo•nee•ohm*
He/She is in a meeting.

Um momento, por favor. *oong moo•mehn•too poor fuh•vaur*
One moment, please.

Sente-se. *sehn•tuh•suh*
Have a seat.

Quer alguma coisa para beber?
kehr ahl•goo•mah coy•zuh puh•ruh beh•behr
Would you like something to drink?

Obrigado m /Obrigada f por vir.
aw•bree•gah•thoo/aw•bree•gah•thuh poor veer
Thank you for coming.

Traveling with Children

ESSENTIAL

Is there a discount for children?	**Há desconto para crianças?** ah dehs•_caun_•too puh•ruh kree•_uhn_•suhs
Can you recommend a babysitter?	**Pode recomendar-me uma babysitter [babá] qualificada?** pawd reh•koo•mehn•_dahr_•meh _oo_•muh bay•bee•sit•tur [bah•_buh_] kwahl•ee•fee•_kah_•duh
Do you have a child's seat/ highchair?	**Pode trazer uma cadeirinha de criança/ cadeira alta?** pawd truh•_zehr_ _oo_•muh kuh•day•_ree_•nyuh deh kree•_uhn_•suh/ kuh•_day_•ruh ahl•tuh
Where can I change the baby?	**Onde posso trocar o bebê [neném]?** aund _paw_•soo _traw_•kahr oo beh•_beh_ [neh•_neh_]

Out & About

Can you recommend something for the kids?	**Pode recomendar algo próprio para crianças?** pawd reh•koo•mehn•_dahr_ ahl•goo _praw_•pree•oo _puh_•ruh kree•_uhn_•suhs
Where's…?	**Onde é…?** aund eh…
the amusement park	**o parque de diversões** oo _pahr_•keh deh dee•vehr•_sohmz_
the arcade	**o salão de jogos** oo suh•_lohm_ deh _zsaw_•gooz
the kiddie [paddling] pool	**a piscina de bebês [nenéns]** uh pee•_see_•nuh deh beh•_behz_ [neh•_nehnz_]
the park	**o parque** oo pahrk
the playground	**o playground** oo _play_•graund
the zoo	**o jardim zoológico** oo zsuhr•_deem_ zoo•_law_•zsee•koo
Are kids allowed?	**São permitidas crianças?** sohm pehr•mee•_tee_•thuhz kree•_uhn_•suhz

| Is it safe for kids? | **É seguro para as crianças?** *eh seh•goo•roo puh•ruh uhz kree•uhn•suhs* |
| Is it suitable for... year olds? | **Será bom para crianças com...anos?** *seh•rah bohng puh•ruh kree•uhn•suhz kaum...uh•nooz* |

YOU MAY HEAR...

Que gracinha/bonitinho!	How cute!
keh grah•see•nyah/boo•nee•tee•nyo	
Qual o nome dele/dela?	What's his/her name?
kwal oo nau•meh dehl/deh•luh	
Quantos anos ele/ela tem?	How old is he/she?
kwuh•tooz uh•nooz ehl/eh•luh teng	

Baby Essentials

Do you have...?	**Tem...?** *teng...*
a baby bottle	**uma mamadeira** *oo•muh muh•muh•deh•rah*
baby wipes	**os lenços umedecidos para o bebê [nenê]** *ooz lehn•sawz oo•muh•duh•see•duhz puh•ruh oo beh•beh [neh•neh]*

a car seat	**um assento de carro** *oong uh·sehn·too deh kah·rroo*
a children's menu/ portion	**uma porção de criança** *oo·muh poor·sohm deh kree·uhn·suh*
a child's seat	**uma cadeirinha de criança** *oo·muh kuh·day·ree·nyuh deh kree·uhn·suh*
a crib	**uma cama de bebê [neném]** *oo·muh kuh·muh deh beh·beh [neh·neh]*
diapers [nappies]	**as fraldas** *uhz frahl·duhz*
formula	**fórmula de bebê [neném]** *fawr·moo·luh deh beh·beh [neh·neh]*
a pacifier [dummy]	**uma chupeta** *oo·muh shoo·peh·tuh*
a playpen	**um parque para crianças** *oong pahr·kuh puh·ruh kree·uhn·suhz*
a stroller [pushchair]	**uma cadeira de bebê [neném]** *oo·muh kuh·day·ruh deh beh·beh [neh·neh]*
Can I breastfeed the baby here?	**Posso amamentar o bebê [neném] aqui?** *paw·soo uh·muh·mehn·tahr oo beh·beh [neh·neh] uh·kee*
Where can I change the baby?	**Onde posso trocar o bebê [neném]?** *aund paw·soo traw·kahr oo beh·beh [neh·neh]*

For Dining with Children, see page 68.

Babysitting

Can you recommend a reliable babsitter?	**Pode recomendar uma babysitter [babá] qualificada?** *pawd reh·koo·mehn·dahr oo·muh bay·bee·sit·tur [bah·bah] kwah·lee·fee·kah·thuh*
What's the charge?	**Qual é o preço?** *kwahl eh oo preh·soo*
I'll be back by...	**Volto às...** *vawl·too ahz...*
I can be reached at...	**Pode me encontrar...** *pawd meh ng·kaun·trahr...*

For Time, see page 175.

Health & Emergency

Can you recommend a pediatrician?	**Pode recomendar um pediatra?** *pawd reh•kau•mehn•dahr oong pee•dee•ah•truh*
My child is allergic to…	**A minha criança é alérgico m /alérgica f a…** *uh mee•nyuh kree•uhn•suh eh uh•lehr•gee•koo/ uh•lehr•gee•kuh uh…*
My son/daughter is missing.	**O meu filho/A minha filha desapareceu.** *oo mehoo fee•lyoo/uh mee•nyuh fee•lyuh deh•zuh•puh•ruh•seoo*
Have you seen a boy/ girl?	**Viu um menino/uma menina?** *veeoo oong meh•nee•noo/oo•muh meh•nee•nuh*

For Health, see page 159.

Disabled Travelers

ESSENTIAL

Is there…?	**Há…?** *ah…*
access for the disabled	**acesso para deficientes físicos** *uh•seh•soo puh•ruh deh•fee•see•ehntz fee•see•kooz*
a wheelchair ramp	**uma rampa de cadeira de rodas** *oo•muh ruhm•puh deh kuh•day•ruh deh raw•thuhz*
a handicapped- [disabled-] accessible toilet	**um banheiro acessível para deficientes** *oong buh•nyay•rooz uh•seh•see•vehl puh•ruh deh•fee•see•ehntz*
I need…	**Preciso de…** *preh•see•zoo deh…*
assistance	**assistência** *uh•see•stehn•see•uh*
an elevator [lift]	**um elevador** *oong eh•leh•vuh•daur*
a ground-floor room	**um quarto no primeiro andar** *oong kwahr•too noo pree•may•roo uhn•dahr*

Asking for Assistance

I'm disabled.	**Sou deficiente.** *sawoo deh·fee·see·ehnt*
I'm deaf.	**Sou surdo** *m* **/Sou surda** *f.* *sawoo soor·doo/sawoo soor·duh*
I'm visually/hearing impaired.	**Vejo/Ouço mal.** *vay·zsoo/ow·soo mahl*
I'm unable to walk far/ use the stairs.	**Não posso caminhar muito/usar as escadas.** *nohm paw·soo kuh·mee·nyahr mween·tuh/oo·zahr uhz ee·skah·thuhz*
Please speak louder.	**Por favor, fale mais alto.** *poor fuh·vaur fah·leh mey·ez ahl·too*
Can I bring my wheelchair?	**Posso trazer a minha cadeira de rodas?** *paw·soo truh·zehr uh mee·nyuh kuh·day·ruh deh raw·duhz*
Are guide dogs permitted?	**Os cães de guia são permitidos?** *ooz kengs de gee·uh sohm pehr·mee·tee·dooz*
Can you help me?	**Pode me ajudar?** *pawd meh uh·zsoo·dahr*
Please open/hold the door.	**Por favor abra/segure a porta.** *poor fuh·vaur ah·bruh/seh·goo·reh uh pawr·tuh*

In an Emergency

Emergencies

ESSENTIAL

Help!	**Socorro!** *soo·kau·rroo*
Go away!	**Vá embora!** *vah ehng·baw·ruh*
Call the police!	**Chame a polícia!** *shuh·meh uh poo·lee·see·uh*
Stop thief!	**Pare o ladrão!** *pah·ree oo luh·drohm*
Get a doctor!	**Chame um médico!** *shuh·meh oong meh·dee·koo*
Fire!	**Fogo!** *fau·goo*
I'm lost.	**Estou perdido** *m* /**perdida** *f.* *ee·stawoo pehr·dee·thoo/pehr·dee·thuh*
Can you help me?	**Pode me ajudar?** *pawd meh uh·zsoo·dahr*

In an emergency, dial **190** for the police, **192** for the ambulance, and **193** for the fire brigade.

YOU MAY HEAR...

Preencha este formulário.
pree·eng·sheh eh·stuh fawr·muh·lah·reeoo

Fill out this form.

A sua identificação, por favor. *uh soo·uh ee·dehnt·tee·fee·kuh·sohm por fuh·vaur*

Your identification, please.

Quando/Onde é que foi? *kwuhn·doo/ aund eh keh foy*

When/Where did it happen?

Como é ele/ela? *kau·moo eh ehleh/ehluh*

What does he/ she look like?

Police

ESSENTIAL

Call the police!	**Chame a polícia!** _shuh·meh uh poo·lee·see·uh_
Where's the police station?	**Onde é a delegacia de polícia?** _aund eh uh deh·leh·guh·see·uh thuh poo·lee·see·uh_
There has been an accident/attack.	**Houve um acidente/ataque.** _auoo·veh oong uh·see·dehnt/uh·tah·keh_
My son/daughter is missing.	**O meu filho/A minha filha desapareceu.** _oo mehoo fee·lyoo/uh mee·nyuh fee·lyuh deh·zuh·puh·ruh·seoo_
I need...	**Preciso de...** _preh·see·zoo deh..._
an interpreter	**um tradutor** _oong truh·doo·taur_
I need...	**Preciso de...** _preh·see·zoo deh..._
to contact my lawyer	**contatar o meu advogado** _kaun·tuh·tahr oo mehoo uhd·voo·gah·thoo_
to make a phone call	**fazer um telefonema** _fuh·zehr oong teh·leh·foo·neh·muh_
I'm innocent.	**Sou inocente.** _sawoo ee·naw·sehnt_

Crime & Lost Property

I want to report...	**Quero reportar...** _keh·roo reh·paur·tahr..._
a mugging	**um assalto** _oong uh·sahl·too_
a rape	**um estupro** _oong ee·stoo·proo_
a theft	**um roubo** _oong rau·boo_
I've been robbed.	**Fui roubado _m_ /roubada _f_.** _fooee raw·bah·thoo/ raw·bah·thuh_

I've been mugged.	**Fui assaltado** *m* **/assaltada** *f.* *fooee uh·sahl·<u>tah</u>·thoo/uh·sahl·<u>tah</u>·duh*
I've lost my…	**Perdi…** *pehr·<u>thee</u>…*
My…has/have been stolen.	**Roubaram a minha/o meu…** *raw·<u>bah</u>·rohm ah minya/ oo maehoo…*
backpack	**a mochila** *uh moo·<u>sheeh</u>·luh*
bicycle	**a bicicleta** *uh bee·see·<u>kleh</u>·tuh*
camera	**a máquina fotográfica** *uh <u>mah</u>·kee·nuh faw·too·<u>grah</u>·fee·kuh*
(hire) car	**o carro (alugado)** *oo <u>kah</u>·rroo (uh·loo·<u>gah</u>·doo)*
computer	**o computador** *oo kaum·poo·tuh·<u>daur</u>*
credit card	**os cartão de crédito** *ooz kuhr·<u>tohm</u> deh <u>kreh</u>·dee·too*
jewelry	**as jóias** *uhz <u>zsoy</u>·uhz*
money	**o dinheiro** *oo dee·<u>nyay</u>·roo*
passport	**o passaporte** *oo pah·suh·<u>pawrt</u>*
purse [handbag]	**a carteira** *uh kuhr·<u>tay</u>·truh*
traveler's checks [cheques]	**os cheques de viagem.** *ooz shehkz deh vee·<u>ah</u>·zseng*
wallet	**a carteira (de documentos)** *uh kuhr·<u>tay</u>·ruh (deh doo·koo·<u>mehn</u>·tooz)*

I need a police report.	**Preciso de um documento da policia.**
	preh•see•zoo deh oong thoo•koo•mehn•too duh
	poo•lee•see•uh
Where is the British/	**Onde fica a embaixada Britânica/Americana/**
American/Irish	**Irlandesa?** *aund fee•kuh uh ehm•beye•shah•duh*
embassy?	*bree•tuhn•nee•kuh/uh•meh•ree•kuh•nuh/*
	eer•luhn•deh•zuh

Health

ESSENTIAL

I'm sick [ill].	**Estou doente.** *ee•stawoo doo•ehnt*
I need an English-	**Preciso de um médico que fale inglês.**
speaking doctor.	*preh•see•zoo deh oong meh•dee•koo keh fah•leh*
	eeng•lehz
It hurts here.	**Dói aqui.** *doy uh•kee*
I have a stomachache.	**Tenho dor de estômago.** *teh•nyoo daur deh*
	ee•stau•muh•goo

Finding a Doctor

Can you recommend	**Pode recomendar um médico/dentista?**
a doctor/dentist?	*pawd reh•koo•mehn•dahr oong meh•dee•koo*
	dehn•teeh•stuh
Could the doctor come	**O médico podia vir aqui me ver?** *oo*
to see me here?	*meh•dee•koo poo•thee•uh veer uh•kee meh vehr*
I need an English-	**Preciso de um médico que fale inglês.**
speaking doctor.	*preh•see•zoo deh oong meh•dee•koo keh*
	fah•leh eeng•lehz

What are the office hours?	**A que horas é a consulta?** *uh kee aw·ruhz eh ah kaun·sool·tuh*
I'd like to make an appointment...	**Queria marcar uma consulta...** *keh·ree·uh muhr·kahr oo·muh kaun·sool·tuh...*
for today	**para hoje** *puh·ruh auyzseh*
for tomorrow	**para amanhã** *puh·ruh uh·muh·nyuh*
as soon as possible	**o mais cedo possível** *oo meyez seh·thoo poo·see·vel*
It's urgent.	**É urgente.** *eh oor·zsehnt*

Symptoms

I'm...	**Estou...** *ee·stawoo...*
bleeding	**sangrando** *suhn·gruhn·doo*
constipated	**resfriado m /resfriada f** *rehz·free·ah·do /oong rehz·free·ah·da*
dizzy	**com tontura** *kaum tohn·too·rra*
I'm nauseous.	**Estou enjoado m /enjoada f.** *ee·stawoo eng·zsoo·ah·thoo/eng·zsoo·ah·thuh*
I'm vomiting.	**Estou vomitando.** *ee·stawoo voo·mee·tahn.do*
It hurts here.	**Dói aqui.** *doy uh·kee*
I have...	**Tenho...** *teh·nyoo...*
an allergic reaction	**uma reação alérgica** *oo·muh rree·ah·sohm uh·lehr·gee·kuh*
chest pain	**dor no peito** *daur noo pay·too*
diarrhea	**diarreia** *dee·uh·rray·uh*
an earache	**dor de ouvidos** *daur deh aw·vee·thooz*
a fever	**uma febre** *oo·muh feh·breh*
pain	**dor** *daur*
a rash	**uma erupção cutânea** *oo·muh eer·oop·sohm koo·tuh·nee·uh*

a sprain	**uma distensão muscular** <u>oo</u>•muh dees•tehn•<u>sohm</u> <u>moos</u>•koo•lahr
some swelling	**um inchaço** oong een•<u>shah</u>•soo
a stomachache	**dor de estômago** daur deh ee•<u>stau</u>•muh•goo
sunstroke.	**uma insolação.** <u>oo</u>•muh een•soo•luh•<u>sohm</u>
I've been sick [ill] for…days.	**Há…dias que me sinto doente.** ah… <u>dee</u>•uhz keh meh <u>seen</u>•too doo•<u>ehnt</u>

For Numbers, see page 173.

Conditions

I'm…	**Sou…** sawoo…
anemic	**anêmico** *m* /**anêmica** *f* uh•<u>neh</u>•mee•koo/ uh•<u>neh</u>•mee•kuh
asthmatic	**asmático** *m* /**asmática** *f* uhz•<u>mah</u>•tee•koo/ uhz•<u>mah</u>•tee•kuh
diabetic	**diabético** *m* /**diabética** *f* dee•uh•<u>beh</u>•tee•koo/ dee•uh•<u>beh</u>•tee•kuh
epileptic	**epilético** eh•pee•leh•tee•koo
I'm allergic to	**Sou alérgico** *m* /**alérgica** *f* **a**

antibiotics/penicillin.	**antibióticos penicilina.** *sawoo uh·lehr·gee·koo/ uh·lehr·gee·kuh uh uhn·tee·bee·aw·tee·kuhz/ peh·neh·seh·lee·nuh*
I have arthritis.	**Tenho artrite.** *teh·nyoo uh·treet*
I have a heart condition.	**Tenho um problema de coração.** *teh·nyoo oong proo·bleh·muh deh koo·ruh·sohm*
I have high/low blood pressure.	**Tenho a pressão arterial alta/baixa.** *teh·nyoo uh preh·sohm uhr·teh·ree·ahl ahl·tuh/beye·shuh*
I'm on...	**Estou tomando...** *ee·stawoo to·muhn·doo...*

YOU MAY HEAR...

Qual é o problema? *kwahl eh oo proo·bleh·muh*	What's the problem?
Onde é que dói? *aund eh keh doy*	Where does it hurt?
Dói aqui? *doy uh·kee*	Does it hurt here?
Toma medicamentos? *taw·muh meh·dee·kuh·mehn·tooz*	Are you on medication?
É alérgico *m* /alérgica *f* a algo? *eh uh·lehr·zee·koo/uh·lehr·zee·kuh uh ahl·goo*	Are you allergic to anything?
Abra a boca. *ah·bruh uh bau·kuh*	Open your mouth.
Respire fundo. *rehs·pee·reh foon·doo*	Breathe deeply.
Tussa, por favor. *too·suh, poor fuh·vaur*	Cough, please.
Quero que vá para o hospital. *keh·roo keh vah puh·ruh oo aws·pee·tahl*	I want you to go to the hospital.

Treatment

Do I need medicine?	**Preciso de algum medicamento?** *preh•see•zoo deh ahl•goong meh•dee•kuh•mehn•too*
Can you prescribe a generic drug [unbranded medication]?	**Pode prescrever um medicamento genérico** *pawd prehz•kreh•vehr oong meh•dee•kuh•mehn•too geh•neh•ree•koo*
Where can I get it?	**Onde posso obtê-lo?** *aund paw•soo au•bteh•loo*

For What to Take, see page 166.

Hospital

Please notify my family.	**Por favor informe a minha família.** *poor fuh•vaur eeng•fawr•meh uh mee•nyuh fuh•mee•lyuh*
I'm in pain.	**Estou com dores.** *ee•stawoo kaun daur•ehz*
I need a doctor/nurse.	**Necessito um médico/uma enfermeira.** *neh•seh•see•too oong meh•dee•koo/oo•muh een•fehr•may•ruh*
When are visiting hours?	**Quais são as horas de visitas?** *kweyez sohm uhz aw•ruhz deh vee•zee•tuhz*
I'm visiting...	**Estou visitando...** *ee•stawoo vee•see•tahn•doo...*

Dentist

I've broken a tooth/ lost a filling.	**Quebrei um dente./Minha restauração caiu.** *keh•bree oong dehnt/minia hes•tahoo•rrah•sohm kah•ee•oo*
I have a toothache.	**Tenho dor de dentes.** *teh•nyoo daur deh dehntz*
Can you fix this denture?	**Pode consertar esta dentadura?** *pawd kaun•sehr•tahr eh•stuh dehn•tuh•doo•ruh*

Gynecologist

I have menstrual cramps/a vaginal infection.	**Tenho dores menstruais/ uma infecção na vagina.** teh·nyoo daurz mehn·stroo·eyez/oo·muh eeng·feh·sohm nuh vuh·zsee·nuh
I missed my period.	**Não tive a última menstruação.** Nohm teev ah ool·tee·mah mehn·strooas·ohn
I'm on the pill.	**Estou tomando a pílula.** ee·stawoo too·muhn·doo uh pee·loo·luh
I'm (not) pregnant.	**(Não) Estou grávida.** (nohm) ee·stawoo grah·vee·thuh
I haven't had my period for...months.	**Já não menstruo há...meses.** zsah nohm mehn·stroo·oh ah...meh·zehz

Optician

I've lost...	**Perdi...** pehr·thee...
one of my contact lenses	**uma das minhas lentes de contato** oo·muh duhz mee·nyuhz lehn·tehz deh kaun·tah·too
my glasses	**os meus óculos** ooz mehooz aw·koo·looz
a lens	**uma lente** oo·muh lehnt

Payment & Insurance

How much?	**Quanto é?** kwuhn·too eh
Can I pay by credit card?	**Posso pagar com cartão de crédito?** paw·soo puh·gahr kaum oo kuhr·tohm deh kreh·dee·too
I have insurance.	**Tenho seguro.** teh·nyoo seh·goo·roo
Can you give me a receipt for my health insurance?	**Podia me dar um recibo para o meu seguro de saúde?** poo·dee·uh meh dar oong reh·see·boo puh·ruh oo mehoo seh·goo·roo deh suh·oo·theh

Pharmacy

ESSENTIAL

Where's the pharmacy [chemist]?
Onde fica a farmácia? *aund fee·kuh uh fuhr·mah·see·uh*

What time does the pharmacy open/close?
A que horas abre/fecha a farmácia? *uh keh aw·ruhz ah·breh/feh·shuh uh fuhr·mah·see·uh*

What would you recommend for...?
O que é que me recomenda para...? *oo keh eh keh meh reh·koo·mehn·duh puh·ruh...*

How much should I take?
Quanto devo tomar? *kwuhn·too deh·voo too·mahr*

Can you fill [make up] this prescription for me?
Pode prescrever esta receita? *pawd prehz·kreh·vehr eh·stuh reh·say·tuh*

I'm allergic to...
Sou alérgico m /alérgica f a... *sawoo uh·lehr·zsee·koo/uh·lehr·zsee·kuh ah...*

Pharmacies (**farmácia**) are easy to find and are often located at main intersections in busy areas. Drugs (**remédios**) are usually quite cheap too as they are subsidised by the government. Pharmacists in Brazil can also make a diagnosis if required and they can also administer vaccinations (**injeção**). For all-night pharmacies (**farmácia de serviço**), you should find the address of the one closest to you displayed in the window.

In the pharmacies in Brazil, you can normally find medicines, perfume, cosmetics and household goods. Travelers who use prescription medicine should bring enough with them to cover their stay.

What to Take

How much should I take?	**Quanto é que devo tomar?** _kwuhn•too eh keh deh•voo too•mahr_
How often should I take it?	**Quantas vezes devo tomar?** _kwuhn•tuhz veh•zehz deh•voo too•mahr_
Is it suitable for children?	**É próprio para crianças?** _eh praw•pree•oo puh•ruh kree•uhn•suhs_
I'm taking...	**Estou tomando...** _ee•stawoo uh too•mahn•doo..._

YOU MAY SEE...

UMA VEZ/TRÊS VEZES POR DIA	once/three times a day
COMPRIMIDO(S)	tablet(s)
GOTA	drop
COLHER(ES) DE CHÁ	teaspoon(s)
ANTES DAS/DEPOIS DAS/COM AS REFEIÇÕES	before/after/with meals
COM O ESTÔMAGO VAZIO	on an empty stomach
INGIRA INTEIRO	swallow whole
PODE CAUSAR SONOLÊNCIA	may cause drowsiness
PARA USO EXTERNO	for external use only

Are there side effects?	**Há efeitos colaterais?** *ah ee-fay-tooz kaw-luh-tehr-eyez*
I'd like some medicine for...	**Queria um remédio para...** *keh-ree-uh oohn ruh-meh-dee-oo puh-ruh...*
a cold	**um resfriado** *oong rehz-free-ah-do*
a cough	**a tosse** *uh taw-seh*
diarrhea	**diarreia** *dee-uh-rray-uh*
a headache	**dor de cabeça** *daur deh kuh-beh-suh*
insect bites	**picadas de insecto** *pee-kah-duhz deh eeng-sehk-too*
motion sickness	**enjoo** *ehn-zsau-oo*
a sore throat	**dor de garganta** *daur deh guhr-guhn-tuh*
sunburn	**queimadura de sol** *kay-muh-doo-ruh deh sawl*
a toothache	**dor de dentes** *daur deh dehnts*
an upset stomach	**uma dor de estômago** *oo-muh daur deh staw-muh-goo*

Basic Supplies

I'd like...	**Queria...** *keh-ree-uh...*
acetaminophen [paracetamol]	**paracetamol** *puh-ruh-seh-tuh-mawl*
antiseptic cream	**pomada antiséptica** *poo-mah-duh uhn-tee-sehp-tee-kuh*
aspirin	**aspirina** *uhz-pee-ree-nuh*
bandages	**umas ataduras** *oo-muhz lee-guh-doo-ruhz uh-tuh-doo-ruhz*
a comb	**um pente** *oong pehnt*
condoms	**preservativos** *preh-sehr-vuh-tee-vooz*
contact lens solution	**um líquido de lente de contato** *oong lee-kee-thoo deh lehnt deh kaun-tah-too*
deodorant	**um desodorante** *oong dehz-aw-doo-ruhnt*

a hairbrush	**uma escova de cabelo** <u>oo</u>·muh ees·<u>kau</u>·vuh deh kuh·<u>beh</u>·loo
I'd like...	**Queria...** keh·<u>ree</u>·uh...
hair spray	**laquê para o cabelo** <u>lah</u>·keh <u>puh</u>·ruh oo kuh·<u>beh</u>·loo
ibuprofen	**ibuprofeno** ee·boo·<u>praw</u>·feh·noo
insect repellent	**repelente para insetos** reh·peh·<u>lehnt</u> <u>puh</u>·ruh een·<u>seh</u>·tooz
a nail file	**uma lixa** <u>oo</u>·muh <u>lee</u>·shah
a (disposable) razor	**gilete (descartável)** zsee·<u>leht</u> (dush·kuhr·<u>tah</u>·vehl)
razor blades	**lâminas de barbear** <u>luh</u>·mee·nuhz deh buhr·bee·<u>ahr</u>
sanitary napkins [towels]	**absorventes higiénicos** uhb·sawr·<u>vehntz</u> ee·<u>zseh</u>·nee·kooz
shampoo/ conditioner	**xampu/condicionador para cabelo** shuhm·<u>poo</u>/ kaun·dee·see·oo·nuh·<u>daur</u> <u>puh</u>·ruh kuh·<u>beh</u>·lo
soap	**sabonete** suh·boo·<u>neht</u>
sunscreen	**protetor solar** praw·teh·<u>taur</u> soo·<u>lahr</u>
tampons	**uns tampões higiênicos** oongz tuhm·<u>poingz</u> ee·<u>zseh</u>·nee·kooz
tissues	**lenços de papel** <u>lehn</u>·sooz deh puh·<u>pehl</u>
toilet paper	**papel higiênico** puh·<u>pehl</u> ee·<u>zseh</u>·nee·koo
toothpaste	**pasta de dentes** <u>pah</u>·stuh deh dehntz

For Baby Essentials, see page 151.

The Basics

Grammar

In Brazilian Portuguese, there are three ways to say 'you' (taking different verb forms): **tu** and **você**.

However, in Brazil, **tu** is hardly ever used. **Tu** refers to just one person at a time, and it takes the second person singular form of the verb.

Você is predominantly used when talking to anyone, regardless of age or class. **Você(s)** takes either the third person singular or the third person plural of the verb depending on whether you're referring to one person (**você**) or more than one person (**vocês**).

The most formal way of saying 'you' is **o(s) senhor(es)** to a man (men) and **a(s) senhora(s)** to a woman (women). **O(s) senhor(es)** and **a(s) senhora(s)** take either the third person singular of the verb or the third person plural depending on whether you're referring to one person (**o senhor/a senhora**) or more than one person (**os senhores/as senhoras**).

Regular Verbs

Here are three of the main categories of regular verbs in the present tense:

	-ar falar (to speak)	-er comer (to eat)	-ir cobrir (to cover)
eu	falo	como	cubro
tu	falas	comes	cobres
ele/ela/você	fala	come	cobre
nós	falamos	comemos	cobrimos
vós	falais	comeis	cobris
eles/elas/vocês	falam	comem	cobrem

Irregular Verbs

In Brazilian Portuguese there are two main verbs meaning 'to be', both of which are irregular.

Ser indicates a permanent state:

Sou inglês.	I'm English.
É portuguesa.	She is Portuguese.

Estar indicates movement or a temporary state:

Está doente.	He is sick [ill].
Estou passeando.	I am walking.

Nouns & Articles

Nouns are either masculine or feminine. Masculine nouns usually end in **-o** and feminine nouns in **-a**. Normally nouns that end in a vowel become plural by adding an **-s**.

Articles must agree with the noun to which they refer in gender and number.

Indefinite: um carro (a car); **uns carros** (some cars); **uma casa** (a house); **umas** casas (some houses)

Definite: o carro (the cars); **os carros** (some cars); **a casa** (the house); **as casas** (the houses)

Word Order

The conjugated verb comes after the subject:

For example:

Maria fala inglês. Maria speaks English.

To ask a question, reverse the order of the subject and verb, change your intonation or use key question words such as **quando** (when).

Quando abre o museu? When does the museum open?

Literally translates to: 'When opens the museum?'

Ela é brasileira? Is she Brazilian?

Literally: She is Brazilian? This is a statement that becomes a question by raising the pitch of the last syllable of the sentence.

Negation

To form a negative sentence, add **não** (not) before the verb. E.g:

Fumamos. We smoke.

Não fumamos. We don't smoke.

Imperatives

Imperative sentences, commands, are formed by adding the appropriate
ending to the stem of the verb.

For example:

Fale! Speak!

Abra a janela, por favor. Open the window, please.

Comparative & Superlative

The comparative is usually formed by adding **mais** (more) or **menos** (less)
before the adjective or noun. The superlative is formed by adding the
appropriate definite article (**o/os**, **a/as**) and **mais** (the most) or **menos** (the
least).

alto	mais alto	o mais alto
tall	taller	tallest
caro	menos caro	o menos caro
expensive	less expensive	least expensive

Possessive Pronouns

Pronouns serve as substitutes for specific nouns and must agree with the noun
in gender and number.

meu *m* /**minha** *f*	mine
teu *m* /**tua** *f*	yours
seu *m* /**sua** *f*	yours (formal)
nosso *m* /**nossa** *f*	ours
vosso *m* /**vossa** *f*	yours (plural)

E.g.: **Esse assento é meu.** That seat is mine.

Adjectives

Adjectives describe nouns and must agree with the noun in gender and number. In Brazilian Portuguese, adjectives usually come after the noun. Masculine adjectives usually end in **-o**, feminine adjectives in **-a**. If the masculine form ends in **-e** (**intellegente**) or with a consonant (**fácil**), the feminine form is generally the same.

For example:

Seu filho/Sua filha é agradável. Your son/daughter is nice.

O mar/A flor azul. The blue ocean/flower.

Adverbs & Adverbial Expressions

Adverbs are used to describe verbs. Some adverbs are formed by adding **-mente** to the singular feminine form of the adjective.

For example:

sincera + mente = sinceramente

The following are some common adverbial time expressions:

agora	now
ainda não	not yet
ainda	still
nunca	never
sempre	always

Numbers

ESSENTIAL

0	**zero** _zeh_·roo
1	**um** *m* /**uma** *f* oong/_oo_·muh
2	**dois** *m* /**duas** *f* doyz/_thoo_·uhz
3	**três** trehz
4	**quatro** _kwah_·troo
5	**cinco** _seeng_·koo
6	**seis** sayz
7	**sete** seht
8	**oito** _oy_·too
9	**nove** nawv
10	**dez** dehz
11	**onze** aunz
12	**doze** dauz
13	**treze** trehz
14	**catorze** kuh·_taurz_
15	**quinze** keengz
16	**dezesseis** dehz·eh·_sayz_
17	**dezessete** dehz·eh·_seht_
18	**dezoito** dehz·_oy_·too
19	**dezenove** deh·zuh·_nawv_
20	**vinte** veent
21	**vinte e um** *m* /**uma** *f* veent ee oong/_oo_·muh
22	**vinte e dois** *m* /**duas** *f* veent ee doyz/_thoo_·uhz
30	**trinta** _treeng_·tuh
31	**trinta e um** *m* /**uma** *f* _treeng_·tuh ee oong/_oo_·muh
40	**quarenta** kwuh·_rehn_·tuh
50	**cinquenta** seeng·_kwehn_·tuh

60	**sessenta** seh·<u>sehn</u>·tuh
70	**setenta** seh·<u>tehn</u>·tuh
80	**oitenta** oy·<u>tehn</u>·tuh
90	**noventa** noo·<u>vehn</u>·tuh
100	**cem** sehn
101	**cento e um** m /**uma** f <u>sehn</u>·too ee oong/<u>oo</u>·muh
200	**duzentos** m /**duzentas** f doo·<u>zehn</u>·tooz/doo·<u>zehn</u>·tuhz
500	**quinhentos** m /**quinhentas** f kee·<u>nyehn</u>·tooz/ kee·<u>nyehn</u>·tuhz
1,000	**mil** meel
10,000	**dez mil** dehz meel
1,000,000	**um milhão** oong mee·<u>lyohm</u>

Ordinal Numbers

first	**o primeiro** m /**a primeira** f oo pree·<u>may</u>·roo/uh pree·<u>may</u>·ruh
second	**o segundo** m /**a segunda** f oo seh·<u>goon</u>·doo/uh seh·<u>goon</u>·duh
third	**o terceiro** m /**a terceira** f oo tehr·<u>say</u>·roo/uh tehr·<u>say</u>·ruh
fourth	**o quarto** m /**a quarta** f oo <u>kwahr</u>·too/uh <u>kwahr</u>·tuh
fifth	**o quinto** m /**a quinta** f oo <u>keen</u>·too/uh <u>keen</u>·tuh
once	**uma vez** <u>oo</u>·muh vehz
twice	**duas vezes** <u>thoo</u>·uhz <u>veh</u>·zehz
three times	**três vezes** trehz <u>veh</u>·zehz

Brazilian Portuguese uses a comma for a decimal point and a period [full stop] or space for thousands, e.g. 4,95; 4.575.000 or 4 575 000.

ESSENTIAL

What time is it?	**Por favor, que horas são?** *poor fuh‑vaur keh aw‑ruhz sohm*
It's noon [mid-day].	**É meio-dia.** *eh may‑oo dee‑uh*
At midnight.	**À meia-noite.** *ah may‑uh noyt*
From nine o'clock to five o'clock.	**Das nove às cinco horas.** *duhz nawv ahz seeng‑koo aw‑ruhz*
Twenty [after] past four.	**Quatro e vinte.** *kwah‑troo ee veent*
A quarter to nine.	**Quinze para as nove.** *kinz puh‑ruh uhz nawv*
5:30 a.m./p.m.	**Cinco e meia de manhã/da tarde.** *seeng‑koo ee may‑uh deh muh‑nyuh/duh tahrd*

In Brazil, time is usually written using the 24-hour clock, e.g. "The movie starts at 17:00". However, when speaking, use the 12-hour clock. For example, 1:00 p.m. is not 13:00 but "**uma hora da tarde**".

Days

ESSENTIAL

Monday	**segunda-feira** seh-_goon_-duh _fay_-ruh
Tuesday	**terça-feira** _tehr_-suh _fay_-ruh
Wednesday	**quarta-feira** _kwahr_-tuh _fay_-ruh
Thursday	**quinta-feira** _keen_-tuh _fay_-ruh
Friday	**sexta-feira** _say_-stuh _fay_-ruh
Saturday	**sábado** _sah_-buh-thoo
Sunday	**domingo** doo-_meeng_-goo

> In Brazil, calendars go from Monday to Sunday. When giving dates, give the day first, then the month, then the year (e.g. 1 May 2009 or 1/5/2014).

Dates

yesterday	**ontem** _awn_-teng
today	**hoje** auzseh
tomorrow	**amanhã** uh-muh-_nuh_
day	**o dia** oo _dee_-uh
week	**a semana** uh seh-_muh_-nuh
month	**o mês** oo mehz
year	**o ano** oo _uh_-noo

Months

January	**Janeiro** zher·_nay_·roo
February	**Fevereiro** feh·_vray_·roo
March	**Março** _mahr_·soo
April	**Abril** uh·_breel_
May	**Maio** _meye_·oo
June	**Junho** _zsoo_·nyoo
July	**Julho** _zsoo_·lyoo
August	**Agosto** uh·_gaus_·too
September	**Setembro** seh·_tehm_·broo
October	**Outubro** aw·_too_·broo
November	**Novembro** noo·_vehm_·broo
December	**Dezembro** deh·_zehm_·broo

Seasons

the spring	**a primavera** uh pree·muh·_veh_·ruh
the summer	**o verão** oo vrohm
the fall [autumn]	**o outono** oo aw·_too_·noo
the winter	**o inverno** oo eeng·_verr_·noo

The dates of **Carnaval** are based on the dates of Lent and Easter, and therefore change every year. **Carnaval** starts on the Saturday before Ash Wednesday and lasts until Ash Wednesday.

Holidays

January 1	New Year's Day
January 6	Epiphany
April 11	Tiradentes Day
May 1	May Day
August 15	Assumption Day
September 7	Independence Day
October 1	Our Lady of Aparecida Day
November 1	All Saints' Day
November 15	Proclamation Day
December 8	Immaculate Conception Day
December 25	Christmas Day

Conversion Tables

When you know	Multiply by	To find
ounces	28.3	grams
pounds	0.45	kilograms
inches	2.54	centimeters
feet	0.3	meters
miles	1.61	kilometers
square inches	6.45 sq.	centimeters
square feet	0.09 sq.	meters
square miles	2.59 sq.	kilometers
pints (U.S./Brit)	0.47/0.56	liters
gallons (U.S./Brit)	3.8/4.5	liters
Fahrenheit	5/9, after 32	Centigrade
Centigrade	9/5, then +32	Fahrenheit

Kilometers to Miles Conversions

1 km – 0.62 mi	**20 km** – 12.4 mi
5 km – 3.10 mi	**50 km** – 31.0 mi
10 km – 6.20 mi	**100 km** – 61.0 mi

Measurement

1 gram	**grama**	= 0.035 oz.
1 kilogram (kg)	**quilo**	= 2.2 lb
1 liter (l)	**litro**	= 1.06 U.S/0.88 Brit. quarts
1 centimeter (cm)	**centimetro**	= 0.4 inch
1 meter (m)	**metro**	= 3.28 ft.
1 kilometer (km)	**quilômetro**	= 0.62 mile

Temperature

-40° C – -40° F	**-1° C** – 30° F	**20° C** – 68° F
-30° C – -22° F	**0° C** – 32° F	**25° C** – 77° F
-20° C – -4° F	**5° C** – 41° F	**30° C** – 86° F
-10° C – 14° F	**10° C** – 50° F	**35° C** – 95° F
-5° C – 23° F	**15° C** – 59° F	

Oven Temperature

100° C – 212° F	**149° C** – 300° F	**204° C** – 400° F
121° C – 250° F	**177° C** – 350° F	**260° C** – 500° F

A

abbey a abadia
able capaz
about a cerca de
above acima
abroad no exterior
abscess o abcesso
accept aceitar
access o acesso
accident o acidente
accidentally sem querer
accommodation o alojamento
accompany acompanhar
accountant contador
activity a atividade
across do outro lado
adaptor o adaptador
address o endereço
admission charge o preço de
   entrada
adult o adulto
aerobics aeróbica
after depois
afternoon tarde
aftershave a loção pós barba

after-sun lotion a loção pós-sol
age a idade
ago há
agree concordar
air conditioning o ar condicionado
air mattress o colchão pneumático
   [o colchão de ar]
air pump a máquina pneumática
   [a bomba de ar]
airline a linha aérea
airmail o correio aéreo
airport o aeroporto
aisle seat o assento de corredor
alarm clock o despertador
alcoholic drink a bebida alcoólica
all tudo
allergic alérgico
allergy a alergia
allow permitir
almost quase
alone sózinho
already já
also também
alter modificar
alternate route o caminho

adj adjective	**BE** British English	**prep** preposition
adv adverb	**n** noun	**v** verb

alternativo

aluminum foil o papel alumínio

always sempre

ambassador o embaixador

ambulance a ambulância

American o americano, a americana

anesthetic a anestesia

and e

announcement anúncio

another outro, outra

answer atender [responder]

antibiotic o antibiótico

antifreeze o anticongelante

antique a antiguidade

antiseptic cream a pomada antiséptica

any algum

anyone else mais alguém

anyone alguém

anything alguma coisa

apartment o apartamento

apologize pedir desculpa

apology a desculpa

appointment a consulta

approximately aproximadamente

archery arco e flecha

architect o arquiteto, a arquiteta

architecture a arquitetura

area a área

area code o código de área

around (the corner) ao virar a

esquina

arrange arranjar

arrivals (airport) chegadas

arrive chegar

art a arte

art gallery a galeria de arte

artificial sweetener o adoçante

artist o/a artista

ashtray o cinzeiro

ask pedir

asleep adormecido, adormecida

aspirin a aspirina

at least pelo menos

athletics atletismo

attack o ataque

attendant o empregado, a empregada

attractive atraente

aunt a tia

Australia a Austrália

Australian o australiano, a australiana

authentic autêntico

authenticity autenticidade

automatic (car) o carro de câmbio automático

automatic teller machine (ATM) o caixa eletrônico

avalanche a avalanche

away longe

awful horrível

B

baby o bebê [neném];
~**sitter** baby-sitter [a babá];
~**wipes** os lenços umedecidos
para o bebê [neném]
baby bottle a mamadeira
back as costas
backache a dor de costas
backpack a mochila
bacon toucinho
bad mau, má
bakery a padaria
balcony a varanda
ball a bola
ballet o ballet [o balé]
band (musical) a banda musical
bandage a atadura
bank o banco
bar o bar
barber o barbeiro
baseball beisebol
basement o porão
basin a bacia
basket o cesto
basketball basquetebol
bath a banheira
bathe tomar banho
bathroom o banheiro
battery a pilha; ~ **(car, computer)**
a bateria
battle site o campo de batalha

be *v* ser; ~ **(temporary
state)** estar; ~ **(location)** ficar
beach a praia
beard a barba
beautiful bonito, bonita
because porque; ~ **of** por causa de
bed a cama; ~ **and breakfast**
pousada [pernoite e café da manhã]
bedding a roupa de cama
bedroom o quarto (de dormir)
bee a abelha
beer a cerveja
before antes de
begin *v* começar
beginner o/a principiante
beginning o começo
beige beige [bege]
belong pertencer
belt o cinto
best melhor
better melhor
between entre
bib o babador
bicycle a bicicleta
big grande
bigger o/a maior
bikini o biquini
binoculars os binóculos
bird o pássaro
bishop o bispo
bite (insect) a picada (de inseto)

bitter azedo
bizarre estranho
black preto
blanket o cobertor
bleach alvejante
blouse a blusa
blow-dry o secador
blue azul
blueberry o mirtilo
board embarcar
boarding (plane) embarque
boarding pass cartão de embarque
boat o barco
boiled cozido
book *n* o livro
book *v* reservar
book of tickets a caderneta de bilhetes
bookstore a livraria
boots as botas
border a fronteira
boring entediante
botanical garden o jardim botânico
bottle a garrafa; ~ **opener** o abridor de garrafas
bowl a tijela
box office a bilheteria
boxing o boxe
boy o menino
boyfriend o namorado

bra o sutiã
bracelet a pulseira
brake *n* o freio
brass o latão
Brazil o Brasil
Brazilian brasileiro
bread o pão
break *v* partir [quebrar]
breakdown avariar [quebrar]
break-in o assalto
breakfast o café da manhã
breathe *v* respirar
bridge a ponte
briefcase a maleta
briefs as calcinhas
brilliant brilhante
bring *v* trazer
Britain a Grã-Bretanha
British britânico
brochure o folheto
bronze o bronze
brother o irmão
brown o castanho
brush a escova
bucket (pail) o balde
build *v* construir
building o edifício
built construído
burger o hambúrguer
burglary o roubo
burnt queimado

bus o ônibus; **~ (long-distance)** o ônibus; **~ station** a estação rodoviária; **~ stop** a parada de ônibus

business class (na) classe executiva; **~ a trip** viagem de negócios

business card o cartão de visitas

busy ocupado

but mas

butcher shop o açougue

butter a manteiga

button o botão

buy v comprar

bye adeus [tchau]

C

cabin a cabine [o camarote]

cable car o funicular; o teleférico

café o café

cake o bolo

calendar o calendário

call v chamar

camcorder a câmera de vídeo

camera a máquina fotográfica; **~ case** o estojo para a máquina; **~ store** a loja de artigos fotográficos

camp v acampar

camping campismo [camping]; **~ equipment** o material de campismo [camping]

campsite o parque de campismo [camping]

can n a lata; **~ opener** o abridor de latas

Canadá o Canadá

Canadian canadense

canal o canal

cancel v cancelar

cancer (disease) o câncer

candle a vela

candy os doces [as balas]

canoe a canoa

canoeing fazer canoagem

canyon o desfiladeiro

car o carro; **~ hire [BE]** aluguel de carros; **~ park [BE]** o parque de estacionamento; **~ rental** aluguel de carros

carafe a jarra

card o cartão ; **ATM ~** o cartão eletrônico; **credit ~** o cartão de crédito; **debit ~** o cartão de débito; **phone ~** o cartão de telefônico

cards as cartas

carpet o tapete

carry transportar

carry-on levar

carton o pacote

cash o dinheiro

cash *v* cobrar
casino o casino
castle o castelo
cat o gato [a gata]
catch *v* **(bus)** apanhar o ônibus
cathedral a catedral
cause *v* causar
cave a caverna
CD o CD
CD-player CD-player, o leitor de CDs
cell phone o celular
celcius celsius
cemetery o cemitério
cent o centavo
certificate o certificado
chair a cadeira
change *n* **(coins)** troco (moeda);
~ *v* **(bus)** mudar (de ônibus);
~ *v* **(clothes)** trocar (de roupa);
~ *v* **(money)** trocar dinheiro;
~ *v* **(reservation)** mudar a
reserva
changing rooms os vestiários
channel (sea) o canal
chapel a capela
charcoal o carvão
charge a tarifa
cheap barato
cheaper mais barato
check (bill) a conta; **put it on the**
~ ponha na conta

check *v* verificar
checkbook o talão de cheques
check-in desk o balcão de registro
check out *v* **(hotel)** pagar a conta
checking account a conta corrente
checkout (supermarket) o caixa
cheers saúde
cheese o queijo
chemical toilet banheiro químico
chemist [BE] a farmácia
chickenpox a varicela
child a criança
child's seat a cadeirinha de criança;
~ **(in car)** a cadeira de criança
chips [BE] as batatas fritas
church a igreja
cigarette o cigarro
cigars os charutos
cinema o cinema
class a classe
clean *adj* limpo [limpa]
clean *v* limpar
cleaner (person) o empregado da
limpeza; ~ **(product)** o produto
de limpeza
cliff a falésia
cling film [BE] o papel aderente
clock o relógio
close (near) perto
close *v* fechar
clothes a roupa; ~ **dryer** a

máquina de secar
clothing store a loja de artigos de vestuário
cloudy nublado
clubs (golf) os tacos de golfe
coast a costa
coat o casaco [comprido]
cockroach a barata
coffee o café
coin a moeda
cold frio; ~ **(illness)** o resfriado
colleague o colega
college o colégio
color a cor
comb o pente
comedy a comédia
comforter o edredom
commission a comissão
compartment (train) o compartimento
compass o compasso; a bússola
complain reclamar
complaint a reclamação
computer o computador
conditioner (hair) o condicionador para o cabelo
condom o preservativo
conductor (orchestra) o maestro
conference a conferência
confirm v confirmar
confirmation a confirmação

connect conectar
connection (flight) conexão
conscious consciente
constipation a prisão de ventre
consulate o consulado
contact v contatar
contact lens as lentes de contacto
contain v conter
contagious contagioso
contraceptive o contraceptivo; anticoncepcional
convenient conveniente
cook o cozinheiro, a cozinheira
cook v cozinhar
cool (temperature) fresco
copper o cobre
corkscrew o saca-rolhas
corn o milho
corner a esquina
correct correto
cost o custo
cot a cama de bebê [neném], o berço
cotton o algodão
cough n a tosse; ~ v tossir
country (nation) o país
countryside o campo
couple (pair) o par
course (meal) o prato
cousin o primo [a prima]
crash n **(car)** a batida [o acidente]

credit card o cartão de crédito;
~ **number** o número do cartão
de crédito

cross v (road) atravessar

crowded lotado; com muita gente

cruise o cruzeiro

crystal o cristal

cup a xícara

cupboard o armário

currency a moeda

currency exchange (office) casa
de câmbio

customs a alfândega; ~
declaration declaração da
alfândega

cut n o corte; ~ v cortar

cycling [BE] o ciclismo

D

daily diariamente

damage danificado

damp úmido

dance n a dança; ~ v dançar;
~ **club** o clube de dança

dangerous perigoso

dark escuro

daughter filha

dawn a madrugada

day o dia

dead morto; ~ **(battery)**
descarregada

deaf surdo

debit card (Port) o cartão de
débito

deck chair espreguiçadeira

declare v declarar

decline o declínio

deduct v (money) deduzir

deep profundo

degrees (temperature) os graus

delay o atraso

delete (computer) apagar

delicatessen a loja de conveniência

delicious delicioso

deliver v entregar

denim o jeans [brim]

dental floss o fio dental

dentist o dentista

deodorant o desodorante

depart v (train, bus) partida

department store loja de
departamentos

departure (train) a partida

depend depende

deposit n o depósito

deposit v depositar

destination o destino

detergent detergente

diabetes o diabetes

diabetic o diabético

diamonds os diamantes

diaper a fralda

diarrhea a diarreia
dictionary o dicionário
diesel o diesel
difficult difícil
digital digital
dining room a sala de jantar
dinner o jantar
direct *adj* direto
direct *v* indicar
direction a direção
directory (telephone) a lista
  telefônica
dirty sujo, suja
disabled (person) o/a deficiente
disconnect (computer) desligar
  [desconectar]
discount o desconto
dish (meal) o prato
dishes a louça
dishwashing liquid o detergente
  para a louça
display case a vitrine
disposable (camera) máquina
  descartável
dive *v* mergulhar
divorced divorciado
doctor o médico
dog o cão
doll a boneca
dollar (U.S.) o dólar
domestic (flight) doméstico

door a porta
double bed a cama de casal
double room o quarto de casal
down abaixo
downstairs em baixo
downtown o centro da cidade
dozen dúzia
dress *n* **(clothing)** vestido
drink *n* bebida
drinking water água potável
drive *v* conduzir
driver condutor
driver's license a carteira de
  motorista
drugstore a farmácia
drunk o bêbado
dry cleaner a lavandaria de limpeza
  a seco
during durante
dusty empoeirado
duty (tax) imposto
duty-free goods a mercadoria
  isenta de impostos
duty-free shopping as compras
  duty-free

E

ear o ouvido
ear drops gotas para os ouvidos
earlier mais cedo
early cedo

earrings os brincos
east leste
easy fácil
eat comer
economy class a classe econômica
electricity a eletricidade
elevator o elevador
e-mail *n* o email; *v* enviar e-mails
e-mail address endereço de e-mail
embassy a embaixada
emerald a esmeralda
emergency a emergência;
~ **exit** a saída de emergência
empty *adj* vazio [vazia]
enamel (jewelry) esmaltaldo
end *v* terminar
engine o motor
England a Inglaterra
English inglês
enjoy *v* apreciar
enough bastante [suficiente]
enter entrar
entertainment entretenimento
envelope o envelope
equipment (sports) o equipamento (esportivo)
erase *v* apagar
error o erro
escalator a escada rolante
essential essencial
e-ticket o bilhete electrônico

EU (European Union) a UE (União Europeia)
euro o euro
Europe a Europa
except exceto
excess o excesso
exchange *v* trocar
exchange rate a taxa de câmbio
excursion a excursão
excuse me (apology) desculpe-me; **(to get attention)** com licença
exhausted *adj* exausto [exausta]
exhibition a exposição
exit a saída
expensive caro
expiration date a data de validade
extremely extremamente
eye o olho

F

face a cara; o rosto
facial a limpeza de pele
family a família
famous famoso
fan (electric) o ventilador
far longe
fare o bilhete
farm a fazenda
fast depressa
faster mais rápido

fast food as refeições rápidas
fat *n* a gordura; *adj* gordo
fat-free sem gordura
father o pai
faucet a torneira
favorite o preferido, a preferida
fax *n* o fax
fax *v* enviar fax
fear o medo
feed *v* alimentar
female a mulher
ferry a balsa
few poucos
fever a febre
field (sports) o campo
fill out *v* **(form)** preencher
film (camera) o filme
fine (penalty) a multa
fire *n* o fogo
fire alarm o alarme de incêndio
fire department [brigade]
  o corpo de bombeiros
fire escape a saída de incêndio
fire extinguisher o extintor de
  incêndio
first o primeiro
first class a primeira classe
first-aid kit o estojo de primeiros
  socorros
fit (clothes) servir
fitting room o provador

fix *v* consertar
flag a bandeira
flash (photography) o flash
flashlight a lanterna
flat (tire) o furo (no pneu)
flight o vôo
floor (level) o andar
flower a flor
fly (insect) a mosca
fly *v* voar
food a comida
football [BE] o futebol
forecast a previsão
foreign o estrangeiro; ~ **currency**
  as moedas estrangeiras
forest a floresta
forget *v* esquecer
fork (utensil) o garfo; ~ **(in road)**
  a bifurcação
form o formulário
formula (baby) a papa
fortunately felizmente
fountain a fonte
free (available) livre;
  ~ **(no charge)** grátis
frequently muitas vezes,
  frequentemente
fresh fresco
friend o amigo, a amiga
full cheio
furniture a mobília; os móveis

G

gallon o galão
game o jogo
garage a garagem [a oficina mecânica]
garbage bag o saco de lixo
garden o jardim
gardener o jardineiro
gasoline a gasolina
gate (airport) o portão
gay club o clube gay
genuine autêntico, autêntica
get out v sair
gift a oferta
girl a menina
girlfriend a namorada
give v dar
give way (on the road) [BE] dar prioridade
glass (drinking) o copo
glass (material) o vidro
glove a luva
go ir
golf o golfe
good bom [boa]; ~ **morning** bom dia; ~**night** boa noite
goodbye adeus
gram o grama
grandparent o avô, a avó
grape a uva
gray o cinza

green o verde
grocery store a mercearia
ground (camping) o terreno
group o grupo
guarantee a garantia
guide (person) o/a guia
guidebook o guia

H

hair o cabelo; ~ **gel** o gel para o cabelo; ~**brush** a escova de cabelo; ~**dryer** o secador de cabelo; ~**spray** o spray para o cabelo
haircut o corte de cabelo
hairdresser (ladies/men) o cabeleireiro (senhoras/homens)
half metade
hammer o martelo
hand a mão
hand cream o creme para as mãos
hand luggage [BE] a bagagem de mão
handbag [BE] a bolsa
handicapped o/a deficiente
handicapped accessible acessível a deficientes
hangover a ressaca
happy feliz
hat o chapéu
have v ter

head a cabeça
health a saúde
hear *v* ouvir
hearing aid o aparelho auditivo
heater o aquecedor
heating [BE] aquecimento
heavy pesado
height a altura
hello oi, olá
help *n* a ajuda
help *v* ajudar
here aqui
high alto(a)
high tide a maré alta
highway a rodovia
hike (walk) o passeio a pé
hiking caminhada
hill a colina
hire *v* [BE] alugar
hire car [BE] o carro de aluguel
hitchhike *v* pedir carona
hitchhiking viajar de carona
hold *v* (contain) conter
holiday o feriado
holiday [BE] as férias
home a casa
horse o cavalo
horseracing a corrida de cavalos
hospital o hospital
hostel o albergue
hot (temperature) quente;

(spicy) picante
hot spring a nascente de água quente
hot water a água quente
hotel o hotel
hour a hora
house a casa
household goods os artigos para a casa
how (question) como
how much (question) quanto
hurt *adj* o ferido, a ferida
husband o marido

I

ice o gelo
ice cream o sorvete;
    ~ parlor a sorveteria; **~ cone** o cone de sorvete
ice hockey o hóquei no gelo
icy *adj* gelado, gelada
identification a identificação
ill *adj* o/a doente
illness a doença
in (place) no; **(time)** em
indoor dentro de casa; **~ pool** a piscina coberta
inexpensive barato
inflammation a inflamação
informal (dress) (o vestido) informal

information a informação
innocent o/a inocente
insect o inseto; ~ **bite** a picada de inseto; ~ **repellent** o repelente de insetos
inside dentro de
insomnia a insônia
instant coffee o café instantâneo
instant message a mensagem instantânea
insulin a insulina
insurance o seguro; ~ **card** a apólice de seguro
interesting interessante
international internacional
internet cafe o cyber café
internet service o serviço de internet
interpreter o/a intérprete
intersection o cruzamento
introduce v introduzir
invite v convidar
Ireland a Irlanda
Irish irlandês
iron v passar a ferro
island a ilha

J

jam geleia
jar o frasco
jeans as calças jeans

jellyfish a água-viva
jewelry as joias
joke a piada
judge o juiz, a juíza
jumper cables os cabos da bateria

K

key a chave
key card o cartão da porta
kiddie pool a piscina de bebês [nenens]
kilo(gram) o quilo(grama)
kilometer o quilometro
kiosk o quiosque
kiss beijar
kitchen a cozinha
knee o joelho

L

lace a renda
ladder a escada
lake o lago
large grande
last o último
late (time) tarde; **(delayed)** atrasado
later mais tarde
launderette [BE] lavanderia automática
laundromat lavanderia automática
laundry service o serviço de

lavanderia
lawyer o advogado, a advogada
learn v aprender
leather o couro
leave v partir
left a esquerda
left-luggage office [BE] o depósito de bagagem
lens lentes
less menos
lesson a lição
letter a carta
library a biblioteca
life a vida
lifeboat o barco salva-vidas
lifeguard o salva-vidas
life jacket o colete salva-vidas
lift [BE] o elevador
light (shade) claro; **(weight)** leve
light n a luz; v ascender
lightbulb a lâmpada (elétrica)
lighter o isqueiro
lightning o relâmpago
line (waiting) a fila (de espera)
line (subway) a linha (do metrô)
linen o linho
lip o lábio
liquor store a loja de bebidas alcoólicas
liter o litro

little pequeno, pequena
live v viver
local regional
lock n a fechadura
locked adj fechado, fechada
locker o armário com cadeado
log on v autenticar
log off v sair
long comprido; **(time)** muito
long-sighted [BE] hipermetrope
look v ver
look for procurar
lose v perder
lost adj perdido
lost-and-found os achados e perdidos
lotion a loção
louder mais alto
love (a person) amar; **(a thing)** gostar de
luggage a bagagem
luggage cart [trolley] o carrinho
luggage locker o guarda-volumes (debagagem)
luggage ticket o cacnhoto do guarda-volumes (de bagagem)
lumpy (mattress) (o colchão) desnivelado
lunch o almoço
lung o pulmão

M

magazine a revista
magnificent magnífico, magnífica
mail o correio
mailbox a caixa do correio
main course o prato principal
make up a prescription
  [BE] receitar
male masculino
man o homem
manager o/a gerente
manicure a manicure
manual (gears) câmbio manual
  (de marchas)
market o mercado
married casado
mass (church service) a missa
massage a massagem
matches (fire) os fósforos
material o material
mattress o colchão
maybe talvez
meal a refeição
mean v significar
measure v medir
measurement a medida
meat a carne
medicine o remédio
medium (size) médio; **(cooked)**
  ao ponto
meet v encontrar(-se)

mend v consertar
menu o menu, o cardápio
message a mensagem
metal o metal
meter (taxi) o taxímetro
meter (parking) o parquímetro
microwave (oven) o microondas
midday [BE] o meio-dia
migraine a enxaqueca
mileage a quilometragem
minibar o frigobar
minute o minuto
mirror o espelho
miss v perder
missing em falta
mistake o engano, o erro
misunderstanding o mal-
  entendido
mobile phone [BE] o celular
mobile home a casa ambulante
modern moderno, moderna
money o dinheiro
monument o monumento
moped a mobilete
more mais
mosquito o mosquito
mother a mãe
motion sickness o enjôo
motor o motor
motorbike a moto
motorboat o barco a motor, a

lancha
motorway [BE] a estrada, a rodovia
mountain a montanha; ~ **bike**
mountain bike
moustache o bigode
mouth a boca
move *v* mudar(-se)
movie o filme
movie theater o cinema
much muito
mug (drinking) a caneca
mugging o assalto
mumps a caxumba
museum o museu
music a música

N

nail (body) a unha; ~**polish** o
esmalte de unhas
name o nome
napkin o guardanapo
nappy [BE] a fralda
narrow estreito
national nacional
nationality a nacionalidade
nature preserve a reserva natural
nausea a náusea
near perto
nearest mais próximo
necessary necessário
neck (body) o pescoço;

(clothing) a gola
necklace o colar
needle a agulha
neighbor o vizinho, a vizinha
nephew o sobrinho
never nunca
new novo, nova
newspaper o jornal
newsstand [newsagent]
a banca de jornais
next próximo, próxima
next to ao lado de
niece a sobrinha
night a noite
nightclub o nightclub
no não
no one ninguém
noisy barulhento
non-alcoholic não-alcoólico,
não-alcoólica
non-smoking *adj* não-fumantes
none nenhum, nenhuma
normal normal
north o norte
note a nota
note [BE] a nota
notebook o caderno
nothing nada
now agora
number (telephone) o número de
telefone

number plate (car) [BE] a placa do carro
nurse o enfermeiro, a enfermeira

O

observatory o observatório
occupied ocupado, ocupada
off-licence [BE] a loja de vinhos
office o escritório
often muitas vezes
oil o óleo
okay O.K.
old o velho, a velha
old-fashioned antigo, antiga
one um, uma
one-way ticket o bilhete de ida
open v abrir
open adj aberto, aberta
opening hours as horas de funcionamento
opera a ópera
operation a operação
opposite o oposto
optician o oculista, oftalmologista
orange (fruit) a laranja; **(color)** laranja
orchestra a orquestra
order v encomendar
outdoor ao ar livre; **~ pool** a piscina ao ar livre
outside fora de

over sobre
overdone adj cozido demais
overnight só uma noite

P

pacifier a chupeta
pack v fazer as malas
package o pacote
paddling pool [BE] a piscina de bebês [nenens]
padlock o cadeado
pain a dor
paint v pintar
painter o pintor, a pintora
painting o quadro
pajamas o pijama
palace o palácio
pants as calças
pantyhose a meia-calça
paper o papel
paper napkin o guardanapo de papel
park o parque
park v estacionar
parking o estacionamento; **~ lot** o parque de estacionamento; **~ meter** o parquímetro; **~ space** a vaga de estacionamento
partner o companheiro, a companheira
part a peça

party a festa
pass n o passe
pass v passar
passenger o passageiro, a passageira
passport o passaporte
pastry shop a doceria [a confeitaria]
patch v remendar
path o caminho
pay v pagar
pay phone o telefone público
peak (mountain) o pico
pearl a pérola
pedestrian crossing a faixa de pedestres
pedicure a pedicure
pen a caneta
pencil o lápis
penicillin a penicilina
per por: ~ **day** por dia; ~ **hour** por hora; ~ **night** por noite; ~ **week** por semana
performance a sessão
perfume o perfume
perhaps talvez
period período
permit a permissão; v permitir
petrol [BE] a gasolina; ~ **station [BE]** o posto de gasolina
pharmacy a farmácia

phone o telefone; ~ **call** o telefonema; ~ **card** o cartão telefônico
photo a fotografia
photocopier a fotocopiadora
photographer o fotógrafo, a fotógrafa
photography a fotografia
pick up v ir buscar; **(collect)** levantar
picnic o piquenique; ~ **area** a área para piqueniques
piece a peça
pill (birth control) a pílula
pillow a almofada
personal identification number (PIN) o PIN
pink cor-de-rosa
piste [BE] a pista; ~ **map [BE]** o mapa de pistas
pizzeria a pizzaria
place o lugar; **(a bet)** apostar
plane o avião
plant a planta
plastic wrap o papel aderente
plate o prato
platform [BE] a plataforma
platinum a platina
play v jogar; **(instrument)** tocar
please por favor
plug (electric) a tomada (eléctrica)

plunger o desentupidor
pocket o bolso
poison o veneno
police a polícia; ~ **report** o boletim de ocorrência da polícia; ~ **station** a delegacia da polícia
pond a lagoa
pool a piscina
pop music a música pop
popcorn as pipocas
popular popular
port (harbor) o porto
Portugal Portugal
Portuguese português
post [BE] o correio; ~ **office** os correios
postbox [BE] a caixa do correio
postcard o cartão postal
poster o pôster
pottery a cerâmica
pound (British sterling) a libra (esterlina)
pregnant a grávida
prescribe receitar
prescription a receita
press v **(clothing)** passar a ferro [engomar]
pretty bonito, bonita
print v imprimir
problem o problema
prohibit proibido

pronounce v pronunciar
public o público
pull v puxar
pump a bomba; **(gas)** a bomba de gasolina
puncture [BE] o furo

Q

quality a qualidade
question a pergunta
queue [BE] n a fila
quiet sossegado, sossegada

R

race (cars, horses) a corrida; ~ **track** o hipódromo
racket (sports) a raquete
railway station [BE] a estação de caminhos de ferro [a estação ferroviária]
rain v chover
raincoat a capa de chuva
rape o estupro
rare (unusual) raro, rara; **(steak)** mal-passado, mal-passada
razor a navalha; ~ **blade** a lâmina de barbear
read v ler
ready pronto, pronta
real (genuine) legítimo, legítima

receipt a fatura [o recibo]
reception (desk) a recepção
receptionist o/a recepcionista
recommend v recomendar
red vermelho, vermelha
refrigerator a geladeira
region a região
regular (gas/petrol) normal
rent v alugar
rental car o carro alugado
repair v arranjar
repeat v repetir
reservation a marcação
reserve v reservar
restaurant o restaurante
restroom o banheiro
return v **(come back)** voltar;
  (give back) devolver
right (correct) certo; ~ **of way**
  prioridade
ring o anel
river o rio
road a estrada
robbed roubado, roubada
robbery o roubo
romantic romântico
room o quarto; ~ **service** o serviço
  de quarto
round redondo, redonda
round-trip de ida e volta
route o caminho

rowboat o barco a remos
rubbish [BE] o lixo; ~ **bin [BE]**
  a lata de lixo, lixeira
ruins as ruínas

S

sad triste
safe n o cofre; adj seguro
safety a segurança
sales tax IVA
same o mesmo, a mesma
sand a areia
sandals as sandálias
sanitary napkin [pad] o papel
  higiênica
saucepan a panela
sauna o sauna
save guardar
savings account a conta de
  poupança
scanner o scanner
scarf o lenço , a echarpe (de
  pescoço)
schedule o horário
school a escola
scissors a tesoura
sea o mar
seat o lugar
see ver
self-service self-service
  [auto-serviço]

sell v vender
send v mandar
senior citizen o idoso, a idosa
separated separado, separada
serious sério, séria
service charge a taxa de serviço
set menu o menu fixo
sex o sexo
**sexually transmitted disease
(STD)**
    Doença Sexualmente Transmissível
    (DST)
shallow pouco fundo, funda
shampoo o shampoo [o xampú]
sharp afiado, afiada
shaving cream o creme da barba
sheet o lençol
ship o navio
shirt a camisa
shoe o sapato; ~ **store** a sapataria
shopping compras; ~ **area** a zona
    comercial; ~ **centre [BE]** o centro
    comercial; ~ **mall** o shopping
    center
short curto
shorts os calções
short sighted [BE] míope
show n o espectáculo; v mostrar
shower o chuveiro
sick doente
side (of road) o lado;

~**effect** o efeito colateral;
~ **order** à parte;
~ **street** transversal
sidewalk a calçada
sightseeing tour o circuito turístico
sign o sinal
silk a seda
silver a prata
single (not married) solteiro; ~
    room
    o quarto individual
sink a pia
sister a irmã
sit v sentar
size o número/tamanho
skin a pele
skirt a saia
skis os esquis
sleep dormir
sleeping bag o saco de dormir
sleeper car [BE] vagão-leito
slice a fatia
slippers chinelos
slope (ski) a rampa
slow lento, lenta
slower mais devagar
slowly devagar
small pequeno, pequena
small change troco
smoke v fumar
smoking (area) zona de fumantes

snack bar a lanchonete, a cafetaria
sneakers os tênis
snorkel mergulho, snorkel
snow a neve; v nevar
snowboard a prancha de snowboard
soap o sabonete
soccer o futebol
sock a meia
soft drink (soda) o refrigerante
sold out esgotada, esgotado
someone alguém
something alguma coisa
sometimes às vezes
son o filho
sore throat a dor de garganta
sorry desculpe
south sul
souvenir a lembrança
spa o spa
speak falar
speed limit o limite de velocidade
speed v ir com excesso de velocidade
spell soletrar
spend gastar
spine a espinha
sponge a esponja
sport o esporte
sporting goods store a loja de esportivos

spring a primavera
square o quadrado
stadium o estádio
stairs as escadas
stamp o selo
start começar
starter [BE] a entrada; o aperitivo
station a estação
station wagon a minivan
statue a estátua
stay permanecer
steal roubar
steep íngreme
sting a picada
stolen roubado
stomach o estômago
stop n **(bus, tram)** a parada
stop v parar
store guide a planta da loja
storey [BE] o andar (do prédio)
straight ahead sempre em frente
stream o riacho
street a estrada
stroller o carrinho de bebê [neném]
student o/a estudante
study v estudar
subway o metrô; ~ **station** a estação de metrô
suit o terno
suitcase a mala de viagem

sun o sol
sun block o protetor solar
sunbathe tomar banho de sol
sunburn a queimadura de sol
sunglasses os óculos de sol
super (fuel) super
supermarket o supermercado
surfboard a prancha de surf
sweatshirt o agasalho, a blusa de moleton
sweet (taste) doce
sweets [BE] os doces, as balas
swim v nadar
swimsuit o maiô de banho
symbol o símbolo
synagogue a sinagoga

T

table a mesa
tablet (medicine) o comprimido
take v **(carry)** levar; **(medicine)** tomar; **(time)** demorar
take away [BE] para levar
tampons os tampões higiênicos
taste v provar
taxi o táxi; ~ **stand** o ponto de táxis
team o time
teaspoon a colher de chá
telephone o telefone
tennis o tênis

tent a tenda; ~ **peg** a cavilha; ~ **pole** a estaca
terminal (airport) o terminal
text v **(send a message)** escrever uma mensagem; n **(message)** mensagem de texto
thank you obrigado m; obrigada f
that esse, essa
theater teatro
theft roubo
there ali
thief ladrão
thigh coxa
thirsty com sede
this este, esta
throat a garganta
ticket o bilhete; ~ **machine** a máquina de venda de bilhetes; ~ **office** a bilheteria
tie (clothing) a gravata
time as horas
timetable [BE] o horário
tire o pneu
tired cansado, cansada
tissue o lenço de papel
today hoje
toe o dedo do pé
together juntos
toilet a casa de banho
toilet paper o papel higiênico
tomorrow amanhã

tongue a língua

tonight hoje à noite; **for ~** para hoje à noite

too (much) demasiado; **(also)** também

tooth o dente

toothbrush a escova de dentes

toothpaste a pasta de dentes

tour a visita

tourist o/a turista

towel a toalha

town a cidade; **~ hall** a câmara municipal; **~ map** o mapa de cidade

toy o brinquedo

toy store a loja de brinquedos

track o trilho

traffic o trânsito; **~ jam** o engarrafamento; **~ circle** o balão; **~ light** o semáforo

trail o caminho; **~ map** o mapa

train o trem; **~ station** a estação ferroviária

transfer (plane, train) a conexão

translate *v* traduzir

trash o lixo; **~ can** a lixeira

travel *v* viajar; **~ agency** a agência de viagens

traveler's check o cheque de viagens

tree a árvore

trip a excursão

trolley o carrinho

trousers [BE] as calças

T-shirt a T-Shirt [a camiseta]

TV a televisão [a TV]

type o tipo

tyre [BE] o pneu

U

ugly feio, feia

umbrella (rain) o guarda-chuva

unbranded medication [BE] o medicamento genérico

uncle o tio

unconscious perder os sentidos

underground [BE] o metrô; **~ station [BE]** a estação de metrô

underpants as cuecas

understand compreende

United Kingdom o Reino Unido

United States os Estados Unidos

university a universidade

unleaded (gas) sem chumbo

unlimited (mileage) sem limite (de quilometragem)

unlock *v* abrir

upper superior

upstairs em cima

use *v* usar

use *n* uso

useful útil
username o nome de usuário
utensil o utensílio

V

vacancy o quarto vago
vacation as férias
vaccination a vacinação
vacuum cleaner o aspirador
vagina a vagina
valid válido
valley o vale
valuable de valor
value o valor
VAT (sales tax) IVA
vegetarian vegetariano
vehicle o veículo; ~ **registration** os documentos do carro
veterinarian o veterinário a veterinária
view point [BE] o mirante
village a aldeia
vineyard o vinhedo
visa o visto
visit n a visita
visit v visitar
visitor center o centro de informações turísticas
visually impaired os deficientes visuais
vitamin a vitamina

volleyball o voleibol
vomit vomitar

W

wait esperar
waiting room a sala de espera
waiter o garçom
waitress a garçonete
wake-up call a chamada para despertar
walk v dar um passeio a pé
walking passear a pé
walking route o roteiro para caminhada
wall a parede
wallet a carteira (de documentos)
warm adj morno, morna; v aquecer
wash v lavar
washing machine a máquina de lavar
watch n o relógio; v ver
water a água
water skis os esquis aquáticos
weather o tempo; ~ **forecast** a previsão do tempo
wedding o casamento; ~ **ring** a aliança de casamento
week a semana
weekend o fim de semana
weekly (ticket) (bilhete) semanal

welcome bem-vindo (m), bem-vinda (f)
west oeste
what o que
wheelchair a cadeira de rodas; ~ **ramp** a rampa para cadeira de rodas
when quando
where onde
white branco, branca
who quem
wife a esposa
window a janela; **(store)** a vitrine
window seat o lugar à janela
windshield o para-brisas
windsurfer a prancha à vela
wireless sem fio; ~ **internet** internet sem fio; ~ **internet service** serviço de internet sem fio; ~ **phone** telefhone sem fio
with com
without sem

woman a mulher
wool a lã
work v **(job)** trabalhar; **(function)** funcionar
wrap v embrulhar
wrist o pulso
write v escrever
wrong errado, errada

Y

year o ano
yellow amarelo, amarela
yes sim
young jovem
youth hostel o albergue da juventude

Z

zebra crossing [BE] a faixa de pedestres
zero zero
zone a zona
zoo o zoológico

Brazilian Portuguese–English

A

à tarde p.m.
a abadia abbey
o abajur lampshade
aberto open
o abraço hug
abril April
acampar camp
o acesso para deficientes access for handicapped
os achados e perdidos lost and found
o açougue butcher
o acrílico acrylic
o açúcar sugar
adiante ahead
as entradas/inscrições admissions
o advogado attorney
o aeroporto airport
a agência de câmbio currency exchange office
a agência de viagens travel agent
agora now
agosto August
a água potável drinking water
o albergue de juventude youth hostel
a aldeia village
a alergia allergy

alérgico allergic
a alfândega customs
o algodão cotton
alguém someone
os alimentos naturais health food
o alojamento accommodations
alpinismo mountaineering
aluga-se for rent
alugam-se carros car rental
aluguel de bicicletas bicycle rental
amanhã tomorrow
a ambulância ambulance
antiguidades antiques
aquecer warm
área para fumantes smoking (area)
a areia sand
o aspirador vacuum
o assento seat
o assento à janela window seat
o assento no corredor aisle seat
a assinatura signature
atender answer
o atendimento admissions
o atendimento ao cliente customer service
atrasado delayed
automático automatic
o automóvel car

o **avião** plane
o **aviso** warning

B

a **bagagem** baggage [luggage]
o **balão** traffic circle [roundabout]
o **balcão de registo** check-in counter
o **balcão de informações** information desk
a **balsa** ferry
a **bancade jornais** newsagent
o **banco** bank
o **banheiro** bathroom [toilets]
a **banheira** bath
o **barbeiro** barber
o **barco** boat
o **barco salva-vidas** lifeboat
o **basebol** baseball
o **basquetebol** basketball
o **beijo** kiss
benvindo welcome
a **biblioteca** library
a **bicicleta** bicycle
a **bicicleta de montanha** mountain bike
o **bilhete eletrônico** e-ticket
o **bilhete semanal** weekly ticket
a **bilheteria** ticket office
o **bilhete** ticket
os **bolsos** pockets
a **bomba** pump

os **bombeiros** fire department [brigade]
o **bonde** tram
as **botas de esqui** ski boots
o **boxe** boxing

C

o **cabeleireiro** hairdresser
o **cabelo** hair
a **cachoeira** waterfall
a **cadeira de rodas** wheelchair
o **café da manhã** breakfast
a **caixa** cashier
o **calçado** shoes
acalculadora calculator
o **calor** heat
as **calorias** calories
a **câmara municipal** municipal town hall
o **caminhão** truck
o **caminho** path
o **camping** campsite
o **campo de esportes** playing field
o **canal** canal
cancelado canceled
o **capacete** helmet
a **capela** chapel
o **cardápio** menu
o **carnaval** carnival
a **carne** meat
o **carro** car

a **carta registrada** registered letter
o **cartão de visitas** business card
a **carteira** wallet
a **casa** house
o **casaco** coat
o **castelo** castle
a **catedral** cathedral
o **cavalo** horse
a **caverna** cave
o **cemitério** cemetery
o **centavo** cent
o **centro da cidade** downtown area
o **centro esportivo** sports center
a **cerveja** beer
o **chá** tea
o **chalé** cottage
a **chamada gratuita** toll-free call
a **chave** key
as **chegadas** arrivals (airport)
a **chupeta** pacifier
o **churrasco** barbecue
a **chuva** rain
o **chuveiro** shower
a **cidade** city
a **cidade antiga** old town
o **cigarro** cigarette
o **cinema** movie theater [cinema]
a **cirurgia** surgery
a **clínica de saúde** health clinic
o **cobre** copper
o **código** code

o **código de área** area code
o **colete salva-vidas** life jacket
a **colina** hill
com with
com chumbo leaded
o **combustível** fuel
completo full
o **comprimido** pill
o **computador** computer
a **comunhão** communion
o **condicionador** conditioner
a **confeitaria** pastry shop
congelado frozen
os **consertos** repairs
a **conta corrente** checking
[current] account
a **conta de poupança** savings
account
o **conteúdo** contents
o **controle de
passaportes** passport control
o(s) **correio(s)** post office
o **correio normal** regular mail
o **correio rápido** express mail
o **cadeado** lock
o **corpo de bombeiros** fire station
os **cosméticos** cosmetics
a **costa** coast
o **couro** leather
o **cartão telefônico** phone card
a **criança** child

o cuidado caution
os cuidados intensivos intensive care

D

a dança dance
a data date
a data de nascimento date of birth
de ida e volta round-trip [return]
a delegacia de polícia police station
o dentista dentist
a depilação a cera waxing
o depósito de bagagem baggage check
descartável disposable
o desconto discount
desembarque arrivals (airport)
o desentupidor plunger
o deserto desert
despachar check (baggage)
o destino destination
o desvio detour [diversion]
o detergente detergent
devagar slow
Dezembro December
dia de Ano Novo New Year's Day
os dias úteis weekdays
os dicionários dictionaries
a dieta diet

digital digital
o dique dam
dirija com cuidado drive carefully
dissolver dissolve
a distância distance
os doces candy [sweets]
os documentos do carro car registration papers
os documentos de registro registration papers
doméstico domestic
domingo Sunday
a dor pain
a drogaria drugstore
a duna dune

E

o elevador elevator
em construção under construction
em uso, ocupado occupied
a embaixada embassy
o embarque departures (airport)
a emergência emergency
empurrar push
a encosta perigosa dangerous slope
o endereço address
a enseada bay
a entrada entrance
a entrada proibida no entry
entrar enter

a entrega de bagagem baggage claim

as entregas deliveries

o equipamento de mergulho diving equipment

os equipamentos eletrônicos electronic goods

a escada rolante escalator

as escadas stairs

escalar climbing

a escola school

o escritório office

a especialidade da casa house specialty

a especialidade da região local specialty

o espectáculo show

o espectador spectator

o esporte sports

o esqui aquático waterskiing

a esquiagem skiing

os esquis skis

os esquis aquáticos water skis

esta noite this evening

a estação station

a estação de trem train station

a estação de metrô subway [underground] station

a estação ferroviária train station

a estação rodoviária bus [coach] station

estacionamento parking deck [car park]

o estacionamento para clientes customer parking

estacione aqui park here

o estádio stadium

a estância turística tourist resort

o estanho can

a estátua statue

a estrada road

a estrada em construção road under construction

a estrada fechada road closed

o estrangeiro foreign

a estreia premiere

o estuário estuary

exclusivo para residentes residents only

exclusivo para pedestres pedestrians only

exclusivo para pessoal autorizado authorized vehicles only

a excursão tour

exige-se a identificação proof of identity required

a exposição exhibition

o extintor (de incêndios) fire extinguisher

F

a fábrica factory
a faixa de ônibus bus lane
a faixa de pedestres crosswalk [zebra crossing]
fala-se inglês English spoken
a falésia cliff
a farmácia drugstore
o farol lighthouse
a fazenda farm
a febre fever
fechado closed
a feira fair
feito à mão handmade
o feriado nacional national holiday
o a ferrovia railroad
Fevereiro February
o fim end
o fim da rodovia end of highway [motorway]
a floresta forest
o/a florista florist
o fogo de artifício fireworks
a fonte fountain
a forma form
a fortaleza fortress
o forte fort
a fotocópia photocopy
a fotografia photography
a fralda diaper [nappy]

o freio brake
o freio de emergência emergency brake
a frente front
fresco fresh
a fronteira border crossing
a fruta fruit
fumar v smoke
o futebol soccer [football]
o futebol americano American football

G

a galeria de arte art gallery
a garagem garage
a garantia guarantee
a gasolina gas [petrol]
genuino genuine
o/a gerente manager
o ginásio gym
o glúten gluten
o golfe golf
a gota drop
gracioso cute
grande large
grátis free
gratuito free
a gravata tie
a grávida pregnant
a grelha de churrasco barbecue
o grelhado grilled

a gruta cave
o guarda chuva umbrella
guardar save
o guia turístico tourist guide
o guia de viagem travel guide

H

o handebol handball
o helicóptero helicopter
o hipismo horseback riding
o hipódromo racetrack [racecourse]
hoje today
o hóquei hockey
o hóquei no gelo ice hockey
o horário schedule [timetable]
o horário comercial business hours
o horário de abertura opening hours
o horário de visitas visiting hours
o hospital hospital
o hotel hotel

I

ida e volta round-trip [return]
a igreja church
a ilha island
a impressão printing
incluído included
incluído no preço included in the price
as informações information

as informações turísticas tourist information
o ingrediente ingredient
o início de rodovia highway [motorway] entrance
inocente innocent
inquebrável unbreakable
inserir v insert
insosso bland
as instruções instructions
integral whole wheat
interdito ao trânsito traffic-free zone
interessado interested
internacional international
introduzir introduce
o inverno winter
o IVA imposto de venda agregada sales tax [VAT]

J

lâmina de barbear razor
Janeiro January
a janela window
o jardim garden
o jardim botânico botanical garden
o jardim de infância kindergarten
a joalheria jeweler
o jogo match
Julho July

Junho June

L

a lã wool
o lago lake
a lancha a motor motorboat
os lanches snacks
a lanterna lamp
os laticínios dairy products
a lavagem de carros car wash
a lavagem de roupa laundry facilities
a lavanderia laundromat [launderette]
a lavanderia a seco dry-cleaner
lavar a seco dry-clean only
lavável à máquina machine washable
a lembrança souvenir
a lente lens
as lições lessons
o limite da cidade city limits
o limite de bagagem baggage allowance
a limpeza cleaning
a língua language
a língua estrangeira foreign language
a linha platform
a linha aérea airline
a linha de bonde tram

a linha férrea railroad [railway]
a linha de pesca fishing rod
a liquidação clearance sale
o líquido liquid
Lisboa Lisbon
a lista telefónica directory
a lista de preços price list
o litoral coast
a livraria bookstore
livre vacant
a lixa nail file
o loção pós-barba after-shave lotion
a loja de alimentos naturais health food store
a loja de antiguidades antique store
a loja de artigos de esporte sporting goods store
a loja de brinquedos toy store
a loja de conveniência delicatessen
a loja de departamento department store
as lojas duty-free duty-free store
esgotado sold out
a loteria lottery
a louça china
o luxo luxury
as luzes highlights

M

a madeira wood
o maestro conductor
Maio May
mais more
mais devagar slower
mais rápido faster
a mamadeira baby bottle
mandar send
os mandriões loafers
o mapa da cidade city map
o mapa dos arredores area map
a máquina fotográfica camera
o mar sea
Março March
as massas noodles
a mata wood
a maternidade maternity
o médico doctor
médio medium
o menu menu
o menu turístico tourist menu
o mercado market
as mercadorias goods
**as mercadorias isentas de
impostos** duty-free goods
a mercearia grocer
mergulhar diving
o metrô subway [underground]
a mina mine
a missa mass

o mobiliário furniture
a moeda coin
o moinho mill
o moinho de vento windmill
molhada wet
o molusco shellfish
a montanha mountain
o montanhismo mountaineering
o monte hill
o monumento monument
**o monumento
comemorativo** (war) memorial
o mosteiro monastery
a moto motorcycle
os móveis furniture
as mudanças manual shift
a troca de óleo oil change
mudar change
a mulher woman
a muralha da cidade city wall
o muro wall
o museu museum
a música music
a música ao vivo live music
a música clássica classical music
a música folk folk music
a música pop pop music

N

nacional national
nacionalidade nationality

nada a declarar nothing to declare
não entre keep out
não fumadores non-smokers
não fumantes non-smokers
não fumar no smoking
não funciona out of order
não-retornável non-returnable
o Natal Christmas
navegação à vela sailing
o navio ship
a neve snow
o nome name
a nome de família last name
o nome de solteira maiden name
Novembro November
novo new
as nozes nuts
o número de telefone telephone number
o número do passaporte passport number

O

as obras construction
o oculista optician
ocupado, em uso occupied
a oferta especial special offer
o óleo oil
o ônibus bus [coach]
o operador operator
a ordem de pagamento money order

a orquestra orchestra
a ourivesaria goldsmith
o ouro gold
o outono fall [autumn]
Outubro October

P

o paço palace
a padaria bakery
o país country
o palácio palace
o palácio da justiça law court
o palco stage
o pão bread
o papel higiênico toilet paper
o papel reciclado recycled paper
a papelaria stationery store
para microondas microwaveable
para uso externo external use only
a parada de ônibus bus stop
o parapente gliding
o pára-quedas parachuting
pare stop
a parede wall
o parque park
o parque de campismo campsite
o parque de diversões amusement park
o parque de estacionamento parking lot [car park]

o parque nacional national park
o parque para clientes customer parking
o parque privativo private parking
as partidas departures (airport)
as partidas internacionais international departures
a Páscoa Easter
o passageiro passenger
as passagens (airplane) tickets
o passaporte passport
o passe mensal monthly ticket
o passeio walkway
o passeio panorâmico scenic route
o passeio a cavalo horseback riding
o passeio com guia guided tour
o passeio circular round trip
a pastilha lozenge
a patinação no gelo ice skating
os patins skates
o patrimônio do estado public (building)
o pedágio toll
pedestre pedestrian
o pediatra pediatrician
a pedicure pedicure
o peito chest
peixaria fish store [fishmonger]
a pensão bed & breakfast
o pedestre pedestrian

pequeno small
o percurso da natureza nature trail
o percurso de bicicleta bike trail
o percurso panorâmico scenic route
perdido lost
o perigo danger
perigoso dangerous
permanecer *v* stay
a pérola pearl
perto near
a pesca fishing
o pico peak
a pílula pill
o PIN PIN
a piscina swimming pool
a pista de corrida racetrack
a pista de ônibus bus lane
pista escorregadia slippery road surface
a pista fechada road closed
a pista simples two-way traffic
a placa do carro license plate [registration] number
o planador gliding
o planetário planetarium
as plataformas platforms
o pneu tire [tyre]
o poço well
pode cozinhar cooking facilities

a polícia police
a polícia de trânsito traffic police
a pomada ointment
o pomar orchard
a ponte bridge
a ponte baixa low bridge
a ponte estreita narrow bridge
a ponte levadiça drawbridge
o ponto de ônibus bus stop
o ponto de táxi taxi stand [rank]
por favor please
a porta door
o porta-moedas purse
a porta de embarque boarding
    gate
a porta de incêndio fire door
o portão gate
a porta automática automatic
    door
o porto port
o posto de ambulância ambulance
    station
o posto de gasolina gas [petrol]
    station
a pousada guest house
o povoado village
a praça town square
a praia beach
a praia de nudismo nudist beach
a prancha de surf[e] surfboard
a prata silver

o prato do dia dish of the day
o preço price
a primavera spring
o primeiro andar first floor
a primeira classe first class
o primeiro nome first name
os primeiros socorros first aid
a prioridade priority
prisão de ventre constipated
privado private
os produtos de limpeza cleaning
    products
proibida a entrada no entry
proibido forbidden
proibido acampar no camping
proibido estacionar no parking
proibido fumar no smoking
a promoção sale
o pronto socorro-emergência
    accident and emergency
o propósito purpose
provar v taste
o próximo next
puxar pull

Q

a quantia fare
quarta-feira Wednesday
o quarto de casal double room
o quarto para alugar room to rent
quatro estrelas four star

a queda de pedras falling rocks
o quilometro kilometer
quinta-feira Thursday

R

os raios-x x-ray
a rampa ramp
a recepção reception
o recibo receipt
reciclado recycled
reduza a velocidade slow down
o reembolso refund
as refeições meals
o regente conductor (music)
a região region
o relicário shrine
a represa dam
reservado reserved
a reserva reservation
o reservatório reservoir
residencial guest house
o restaurante restaurant
retirada de dinheiro withdraw
   money
retire o bilhete take ticket
retornar v return
a revista magazine
a ribeira stream
o rio river
o rochedo cliff
a rodovia highway [motorway]

o rolo film (camera)
a rota alternada alternate route
roupa íntima underwear
a rua street
rua estreita narrow road
a rua fechada ao trânsito road
   closed
a rua principal main road
a rua com sentido único one-way
   street
as ruinas ruins

S

sábado Saturday
o sabonete soap
o saco bag
a saída exit
a saída de emergência
   emergency exit
o sal salt
a sala de operações
   operating room
a sala de concertos concert hall
a sala de espera waiting room
o salva-vidas lifeguards
o sapato shoe
a sé cathedral
o secador de cabelo hair dryer
a seda silk
a segunda classe second class
o segundo andar second floor

segunda-feira Monday
os segundos seconds
a segurança security
o seguro insurance
o selo stamp
sem açúcar sugar-free
sem álcool alcohol-free
sem cafeína caffeine-free
sem chumbo unleaded
sem gordura fat-free
sem sal salt-free
o semáforo traffic light
a semana week
a senha ticket
as senhoras ladies
a serra mountain range
o serviço service charge
o serviço a clientes customer service
o serviço de emergência emergency serviceso
o serviço de quarto room service
o serviço incluído service included
Setembro September
sexta-feira Friday
o shopping center shopping mall [shopping centre]
o silêncio silence
a sinaleira traffic light
só com dinheiro cash only
a sobremesa dessert

a soirée evening performance
o solário sun lounge
a sopa soup
o spa spa
o suco fruit juice
o supermercado supermarket

T

os talheres utensils [cutlery]
a tarifa rate
a tarifa de pedágio toll
a tarifa mínima minimum charge
a taxa de serviço service charge
o táxi taxi
o taxímetro taxi meter
o teatro theater
o teatro ao ar livrea open-air theater
o teatro infantil children´s theater
o teleférico chair lift
o telefone telephone
o telefone de emergência emergency telephone
o telefone público public telephone
o telefone residencial home phone number
os temperos spices
a tenda tent
o tênis tennis
a terapia intensiva intensive care

terça-feira Tuesday
o terminal terminal
tinta fresca wet paint
as toalhas linen
tóxico toxic
o tráfego lento slow traffic
o trailer/reboque trailer
o trajeto de ônibus bus route
o trampolim diving board
transferir transfer
o trânsito impedido closed to traffic
transportar carry
o tratamento treatment
o trem expresso express train
o trem local local train
o trem metropolitano local train
o trem rápido express train
trevo, cruzamento intersection
o trigo wheat
o túmulo grave
o túnel tunnel
o turismo tourist information office

U

a universidade university
os utensílios de cozinha kitchen equipment
os utensílios domésticos household goods

V

o vagão-leito sleeping car
o vagão restaurante dining car
a vaga vacancy
vago vacant
o vale valley
o vale postal money order
válido valid
a varanda balcony
os vegetais vegetables
o veículo vehicle
o veículo lento slow vehicle
o veleiro sailboat
a velocidade máxima maximum speed limit
venenoso poisonous
o verão summer
o verdadeiro real
o verdureiro fruit and vegetable store
o vestuário fitting room
a via de dois sentidos two-way traffic
a via de sentido único one-way street
a via turística scenic route
o vidro glass
o vidro reciclado recycled glass
a vila town
o vilarejo village
as vinhas vineyard

o **vinho do porto** port (wine)
o **vinho** wine
a **visita guiada** guided tour
o **voleibol** volleyball
o **vôo** flight

Z

o **zoológico** a zoo
  aduaneira customs zone

a **zona** a zone
a **zona comercial**
  business district
a **zona de pedestres** pedestrian
  zone
a **zona histórica** historic area
a **zona residencial**
  residential zone
zero zero

Berlitz®

speaking your language

phrase book & dictionary
phrase book & CD

Available in: Arabic, Burmese*, Cantonese Chinese, Croatian, Czech*, Danish*, Dutch, English, Filipino, Finnish*, French, German, Greek, Hebrew*, Hindi*, Hungarian*, Indonesian, Italian, Japanese, Korean, Latin American Spanish, Malay, Mandarin Chinese, Mexican Spanish, Norwegian, Polish, Portuguese, Romanian*, Russian, Spanish, Swedish, Thai, Turkish, Vietnamese

*Book only

www.berlitzpublishing.com